The Earp Clan

The Earp Clan:
The Southern California Years

Nicholas R. Cataldo

iv

JM

ISBN: 0-9788187-09

Printed in the United States of America
by Jostens of Visalia, California

Set in 12 point Palatino Linotype
Cover: Cover photograph from a painting by Mike Bennett
Cover design by Ron McKinley, http://southwestsavvy.com
Cover art work by Maggie Heyn.

Library of Congress Control Number: 2006933050

Library of Congress Cataloguing-in-Publication

1. California History

2. Biography

3. San Bernardino County History

4. American West

5. Famous Americans

6. Mining

Includes Index

A Publication of Back Roads Press
6804 N. Ventura Court
San Bernardino, CA 92407
yankeenut@excite.com

DEDICATION

To my wonderful family for always encouraging and supporting my passion for history: my parents, John and Frances; my son, Jay; and especially to Linda, my loving wife of nearly 20 years. With love and affection. —Nick

Table of Contents

PREFACE

During one of my visits to Tombstone some years back, I really took notice how much in common that famous Arizona silver mining town had with San Bernardino, California.

While strolling down Tombstone's Allen Street, I gazed at the wonderfully preserved establishments that have added so much color to the "Town Too Tough to Die". The thought came to me that if San Bernardino's leadership of yesteryear had done things a bit differently, that town could have been preserved as a Wild West tourist attraction.

Tombstone, notorious for its rowdy mining camp reputation during it's hey day, had such honky-tonk establishments as the Bird Cage Theater, the Crystal Palace and the Oriental Saloon. San Bernardino, a supply center for the gold mining ventures at Holcomb Valley, was noted during the same time period for its "Whiskey Point" at 3rd and "D" Streets — so named because it had saloons at each corner.

While Tombstone with its thriving China Town was infamously remembered for its prostitution district, San Bernardino's "Red Light" district on D Street just below the city limits, was pretty darn notorious. San Bernardino also had a flourishing China Town on the north side of 3rd Street between Arrowhead Avenue and Sierra Way.

Tombstone went through a period when the surrounding area was haunted by a notorious Apache

Indian chief—Geronimo—whose raids necessitated the establishment of Fort Huachuca. And there was a time when San Bernardino was so frequently raided by horse thieves led by a much-feared Ute Indian Chief named Wakara, that the Mormon settlers lived in Fort San Bernardino.

Tombstone was best known for its tough reputation with outlaws such as the Clantons, the McLaurys, Johnny Ringo and Curly Bill Brocius. To protect the town's citizens, there were such well known names like Bat Masterson, Doc Holliday, Luke Short and of course, the Earp boys.

San Bernardino also had its outlaw element— "Hell Roaring" Johnson, the Mason-Henry Gang, the Button Gang, and the "El Monte Boys". Its town folk were protected by men like Ben Mathews, Rube Herring, John Ralphs—and for a short time, the Earp boys.

The story of the Earps lives on in books, movies, and even a 1950s television series. The focus has always been on their "lawman" escapades in Tombstone. The truth is they lived there just a little over two years. And what is not well known is that the entire family spent most of their time in Southern California's San Bernardino County.

The Earp Clan: The Southern California Years is the story of the legendary family's many years living in San Bernardino County. I hope you enjoy it.

—Nick Cataldo

ACKNOWLEDGMENTS

Putting this book together was possible only because of the incredible amount of help I received. I would need an entire book in order to list every individual. Hoping that nobody feels left out, I can only acknowledge a small portion of these wonderful people.

I would like to thank two very dear friends who passed on some years ago who were very influential in getting me involved with researching the Earp family—Award winning San Bernardino County Historian, Arda Haenszel, who was always generous about opening her incredible files for me and Fred Holladay, who did a considerable amount of research on the Earps during their stay in San Bernardino County.

I am very grateful to several Earp historians who have been a tremendous help for me. Glenn G. Boyer, who has spent decades researching the Earps, was always very open about sharing his vast knowledge with me. Jim Petersen gave me some valuable information on Wyatt Earp's days with the Los Angeles Police Department. Ben Traywick, Lee Silva and Michael Hickey were also very gracious with their time, information and encouragement.

A huge portion of research done in preparation for this book was gathered from the San Bernardino Historical and Pioneer Society; the "California Room", which is located in San Bernardino's Norman Feldheym Central Library; the Colton City Library; and the San Bernardino County Archives.

The wonderful personal interviews with Grace Spolidoro and her niece, Elena Armstrong, Al Bessant, Robert Clyde, Jack H. Brown and the late John Earp, gave me insightful knowledge on the Earp clan.

A big thanks also goes to Richard Molony, a descendant of the Rousseau family; genealogist Marsha Patrick; Mike Stubbs, who took me out to Wyatt's desert camp; Serena Steiner, interpretive program coordinator at Calico Ghost Town; and local historians from San Bernardino County—Larry Sheffield, Tom Atchley, Peggy Christian, and the late Hazel E. Olson.

Other people who helped make this book possible were Joan Roberts, a descendant of Nicholas Earp's third wife; Steve Shaw, President of the San Bernardino Historical and Pioneer Society; Suzie Earp, Historian Archivist at California State University, San Bernardino; Mike Bennett, who provided the art work for the book cover; and Ron McKinley, who did the book design and layout.

R. W. Waterman in front of his office at the Waterman Mine near Waterman Junction, California (now present-day Barstow, California. Waterman would play a big part in the history of San Bernardino County, the State of California and the Earp Clan—especially Virgil Earp. From the Mojave River Valley Museum Collection.

Virgil Earp's Gold Furnace taken at Calico Mining Camp. There is no record of Virgil ever visiting Calico but brother Jim Earp and his wife Bessie visited there in late April of 1885, and may have taken it there to sell. Calico was a silver mining camp but small quanties of gold and other metals were also recovered. Photo from the Mojave River Valley Museum Collection.

Chapter One

DIARY OF THE EARP WAGON TRAIN
TO SAN BERNARDINO

&

There were many diaries kept by pioneer women trekking West with their families. One of those was written by a woman traveling by wagon train from Iowa to Southern California's San Bernardino Valley, a seven month journey through rugged mountains and across barren plains and deserts. This is known as the Rousseau Diary.

Sarah Jane Rousseau from the Richard Molony Collection.

Born into a well-to-do English family in1816, Sarah Jane Daglish blossomed into a highly educated woman. She was home-schooled by accomplished tutors. In fact, one was a music instructor who had been mentored by a fairly decent classical composer by the name of Ludwig Van Beethoven.

Upon arrival in America, Sarah Jane lived for a while in Michigan. There she met her future husband, a promising young physician named James A. Rousseau.

As newly weds, the couple moved on to Kentucky in 1839

before finally settling down in Knoxville, Iowa, where they raised four children.

From Iowa the Rousseaus and three neighboring families—the Earps, the Curtises, and the Hamiltons—moved out west.

Suffering from a debilitating case of rheumatism, Sarah Jane was eager to escape from the bitter cold Iowa winters. Perhaps she could find relief from her crippling disease at her new home.[1]

On May 12, 1864, the four families embarked by wagon train for Southern California, rendezvousing at the nearby town of Pella, where wagon master Nicholas Earp and his family lived. Sarah Jane Rousseau, virtually unable to walk by this time, began her wonderful journal of the group's experiences which eventually took them to the town of San Bernardino. Her diary was detailed with descriptions of the caravans' day-to-day life.

After spending the first couple nights at the Rousseau's old home town of Knoxville, the travelers expressed their euphoria early on.

The "Rousseau Diary" tells us:

Monday May 16th: Got up and prepared breakfast. After eating all confusion getting ready to start. I can't describe the appearance of all things as they really are. But the weather is indeed beautiful. All nature seems smiling. The birds singing their lively song of praise unto Most High God We started and went through

Sandyville, then as far as the lower River, about ten miles from Pleasantville. So here we camped for the night. Just done eating supper and getting ready for bed. The girls are talking of fishing some tonight. Elizabeth and Mattie have been riding horseback most of the day. John has been riding his mare most of the time and Albert most of his.

Elizabeth, John, and Albert were the writer's children. Mattie seems to have been accompanying the family on the trip.

Tuesday, May 17th: We did not get off this morning as I thought we should. We were detained on account of Jesse Curtis's cow running off. I hope he will be here tonight. Jesse has come. Could not find his cow and now one of his horses has run off. Tom has started after her. He had to go to the other side of Pleasantville about one mile before he got her. Some man saw her and put her in a stable.

Later during the journey men encountered along the trail were not always so apt to be honest and obliging.

She noted when the caravan reached Council Bluffs they'd made 163 miles, an average of about twelve miles a day. [Pretty tolerable speed considering the condition of roads back then.]

The party's first major mishap occurred as they crossed the Missouri River when little Allen Curtis fell from a mule wagon which ran over him. Fortunately, the lad survived.

Sarah Jane wrote lyrically about almost everything between throughout the trip: rivers, birds, grass, thunderstorms, wind, distances traveled, Indians, members of the party being sick, etc.

Her diary mentions that on June 6th the group met up with a Pawnee Indian who wanted soap and matches. The next day, they encountered quicksand for the first time. And before long, they began to encounter a number of graves—so often commented on by every plains traveler.

While the wagon train was cautiously working through Lakota Indian country, Sarah Jane mentioned using buffalo chips for fuel for the first time. By then she also had reported a murdered body discovered by Nick Earp, a drowning, and an eighteen year old boy killed during a horse stampede.

The balance of the trip was frequently a nasty ordeal. Lack of discipline between the families often led to a frequent bickering and little cooperation.

Mrs. Rousseau's comments also shed some light on the abrasive personality of wagon master, Nick Earp, throughout the trip.

While resting at Fort Laramie on July 7th and 8th, she commented that "we have to keep close watch day and night over the stock. Mr. Earp went out to see about the guards (military guards) and found they had got up a dance. And he told them they must quit their dancing and be on duty. One of the soldiers told him to mind his own business and ordered him off. It made him awful mad and he was for killing. He used very profane language; he could hardly be appeased. But he cooled down after awhile and all was quiet."

As the long and exhausting wagon trip met up with the dead heat of summer, dissension within the traveling party reached new heights. Of course, Nick Earp's cantankerous demeanor didn't help.

Prior to stopping at Fort Bridger, the Rousseau Diary for July 30 reported that "... Earp got angry with the whole train because they passed him, he took it as an insult, talked pretty hard to all, some thought he had taken a little too much liquor. He used very profane language and told the whole train that he would give up his Captaincy unless they would adhere to the rules he gave. After being detained an hour or more very unpleasantly we rolled on..."

In another entry, written near Las Vegas on November 10, 1864, she remarked:

> We fed five (Indians) among us. All were willing to do so but Mr. Earp. he swears and cuts up about it, although he derives the same benefit as the rest of us.

Again on November 24th, she commented:

> This evening Mr. Earp had another rippet with Warren (The youngest Earp son) fighting with Jimmy Hatten. And then he commenced about all the children. Used very profane language and swore if the children's parents did

not correct their children he would whip every last one of them. He still shows out more and more every day what kind of man he is.

Sarah Jane happily noted in her diary upon reaching hot dry weather while traveling further west, that she was finally feeling better. In fact, the pioneer woman was now able to walk without the help of a chair which she had been forced to do while enduring cold

Author standing on part of the old road in Cajon Pass where the Earp Caravan passed enroute to San Bernardino. 1986 view.

weather.

On Saturday, December 17, 1864, her final entry read:

A very cold freezing morning. The ground covered with snow. Started up from camp about an hour before day, got to the top of the Sierra Nevada Mountains by daylight. From the foot of the mountain to the top of the Sierra Nevada Mountains (Cajon Pass). Then we went down a very steep hill, it is down hill all the way to San Bernardino. We are now at Martin's ranch

(near present-day Glen Helen Park in Devore), the appearance of the country is quite different from what it has been for sometime back. Everything has a green lively look. The grass growing nicely, it looks like spring instead of the middle of winter. Got into San Bernardino about sun down. I don't know yet if we'll remain here or not. I haven't seen the town yet. Don't know how it looks. I wish to get settled down.[2]

Israel C. Curtis of the 1864 Rousseau Diary. He helped start First Baptist Church of San Bernardino in 1866 and served as its pastor from 1866 until 1868.

Indeed, the Rousseau's did settle down in San Bernardino. In fact several members of the wagon caravan from Iowa became celebrated in the early history of San

Bernardino County.

Nicholas Earp, father of the well known Earp brothers, served as city recorder and justice of the peace in the young town of Colton.

Israel Curtis founded the first Baptist Church in San Bernardino. And both his grandson and great grandson became prominent attorneys and federal judges in the area.

Dr. James Rousseau from the Richard Molony Collection.

In addition to his work as a physician, James Rousseau established a successful career as a surveyor and served as County Superintendent of Schools during the late 1870s.[3]

Perhaps the most dramatic pioneer exploits of all, however, belong to Sarah Jane Rousseau, who became a well-known piano teacher in San Bernardino and gave lessons until her passing on February 20, 1872, at the age of 56.[4,5]

Although Sarah Jane has been gone for well over a century, her wonderful diary lives on. In fact, the San Bernardino County Museum Association included a portion of her journal—from Salt Lake to San Bernardino—in one of its quarterly publications back in 1958.

Third Street in downtown San Bernardino looking east from "D" shows how a part of the "Old West" the town was in 1864. Author's Collection.

Grave of Mrs. J. Rousseau in Pioneer Cemetery in San Bernardino.

Nicholas R. Cataldo

END NOTES

1. Molony, Richard, Oral Interview, 1998.

2. Rousseau, Sarah Jane, Rousseau Diary, 1864.

3. Smith, Dr. Gerald A., *San Bernardino County Museum Association Quarterly*, Vol. VI, winter, 1958.

4. *San Bernardino Guardian* (newspaper), May 23, 1868, p. 2, col. 1.

5. *San Bernardino Guardian*, (newspaper), February 24, 1872.

Chapter Two

PATRIARCH OF THE EARP CLAN
NICHOLAS PORTER EARP

Much has been written about the legendary Earp brothers. Their escapades in Wichita, Dodge City and Tombstone are well known. Little however, has ever been mentioned about their colorful father, Nicholas Porter Earp, who led a pretty adventurous life himself.

Nick Earp when he was 65. Photo courtesy San Bernardino Historical and Pioneer Society.

Described by family members as both religious yet profane and viewing the world that he lived in as black and white, "Nick" knew only two kinds of people—friends and enemies. His friends could do no wrong while his enemies could do absolutely nothing right.[1]

The third of nine children born to Walter and Martha Earp, Nick was born in Lincoln County, North Carolina, on September 6, 1813. His siblings included Lorenzo Dow, 1809; Elizabeth, 1811; Josiah Jackson, 1816; James O'Kelley, 1818; Francis Asbury, 1821; Walter C. (twin), 1824; Jonathan Douglas (twin), 1824; and Sally Ann, 1826.[2]

When he was 23 years old and living in Hartford, Kentucky, Nick began courting Abigail Storm and the two were married on December 22, 1836. Their first born child was Newton Jasper on October 7, 1837. A girl, Mariah Ann was born on February 12, 1839, but lived less than a year. She was predeceased by her mother who died on October 8, 1839 at the age of twenty six.

Nick didn't stay a widower very long though and married nineteen year old Virginia Ann Cooksey (1821 to 1893) on July 30, 1840. This one lasted 53 years and their children were:

James Cooksey (1841-1926)
Virgil Walter (1843-1905)
Martha Elizabeth (1845-1856)
Wyatt Berry Stapp (1848-1929)
Morgan Seth (1851-1882)
Warren Baxter (1855-1900)
Virginia Ann (1858-1861)
Adelia Douglas (1861-1941)[3]

Short (5' 8") and stocky, Nick was a jack of all trades. As a young man he farmed in Kentucky, captained a river boat in Iowa and became an expert cooper. In 1847 he served as a cavalry sergeant in the Mexican War and in 1863 was appointed assistant provost marshal in charge of recruitments for the Union Army. He also dabbled in politics, farming, and was at times a lawman.[4]

In 1845, Nick and Virginia took their budding family to Monmouth, Illinois. A couple years later when the war with Mexico was heating up, he began serving with a company of Illinois Mounted Volunteers. His service would eventually determine the name of his son, "Wyatt Berry Stapp" Earp, for Nick's commander in the war.

Nick was mustered in at Quincy, Illinois, on August 6, 1847, and was discharged with the grade of sergeant on December 24 of that year. His pension claimed that he was kicked by a mule, which caused a lifelong disability from a hernia.[5]

Earp claimed in later years to the San Bernardino Society of California Pioneers that he left his growing family in Iowa and joined in with the gold rush in Northern California. After months of back breaking work and frustration picking away in the mines near Hangtown (now Placerville) in 1851, the frustrated prospector was more than ready to head back home.[6]

On the return trip Nick crossed the beautiful San Bernardino Valley in Southern California and vowed that someday he would make it back to this wonderland of lush fertile fields, boundless timberlands, and deep, clear water streams. And he would do just that.

Rendezvousing out of Pella, Iowa where he had served for a while as town marshal and most recently as assistant provost marshal, Nick led a wagon train consisting of four families—the Rousseau, Curtis, Hamilton, and Earp clans—to the San Bernardino Valley. Included in the group was his wife Virginia, sons Wyatt (16 years old) James, Morgan, Warren, and 3-year-old daughter Adelia. Another son, Virgil, was still serving in the Union army and rejoined them a short time later.[7]

According to Jesse Curtis, great-grandson of one of the party, the train started out with 30 people. Three children were born to the other families later during the journey.

Mrs. Sarah Jane Rousseau, who kept a diary of the trip, mentioned that after they made their first night's camp, seven more wagons straggled in late. By the time the wagon train reached its destination there were about a dozen wagons in all.

Nick Earp proved to be a tough no—nonsense individual who wasn't always so easy to get along with as Rousseau emphatically documented. In her diary of the long journey, Sarah Jane wrote lyrically about almost everything: rivers, birds, grass, thunderstorms, distances traveled, Indians, members of the party getting sick. She also shed some light on the sometimes abrasive personality of their wagon master.

While resting at Fort Laramie on July 7th and 8th, Sarah Jane commented that "we have to keep close watch out to see about the guards (military guards) and found they had got up a dance. And he told them they must quit their dancing and be on duty. One of the soldiers told him to mind his own business and ordered him off. It made him (Nick) awful mad and he was for killing. He used very profane language; he could hardly be appeased. But he cooled down after awhile and all was quiet."

As the long and exhausting wagon excursion met up with the dead heat of summer, dissension within the traveling party got pretty tense at times. Of course, Nick Earp's cantankerous demeanor didn't help.

Prior to stopping at Fort Bridger, the Rousseau Diary for July 30 reported that "... Earp got angry with the whole train because they passed him, he took it as an insult, talked pretty hard to all, some thought he had taken a little too much liquor. He used very profane language and told the whole train that he would give up the Captaincy unless they would adhere to the rules he gave. After being detained an hour or more very unpleasantly we rolled on..."

The seven month journey finally came to an end when the caravan arrived in San Bernardino on December 17.[8]

According to Holman Curtis, one of the young children in the party, the families set up camp just east of today's San Bernardino County Courthouse. The town that greeted them was pretty tough. San Bernardino featured a number of saloons, gambling halls, and a flourishing red light district on south "D" Street. It also proved to be Nick Earp's kind of town.[9]

NOTORIOUS "D" STREET

During the 1860s, the corner of Third and "D" in

San Bernardino was infamously known as Whiskey Point—because it hosted saloons at each corner. And with a flourishing "Red Light District" just south of the

Third Street in downtown San Bernardino looking east from "D" shows how a part of the "Old West" the town was in 1864. Saloons stood at each corner of that intersection, prompting the interesting moniker "Whiskey Point." Author's Collection.

city limits, when it came to entertainment of the bawdy sort, the place to be (or avoid) was the notorious "D" Street.

George A. Atwood, who came to the city at the age of 7 in 1860, recalled his childhood memories of the town during a speech he gave before the local Lion's Club in 1935. Here is what he had to say:

"San Bernardino was but a little town when we arrived here. I remembered they claimed about 500 people altogether, Mexicans, Indians, and whites".

"The business of the town was little and was mostly done on four corners: Fourth Street and Arrowhead Avenue, which was then known as "C" Street (Lewis Jacobs' and Calisher's general stores); the corner of Third and Arrowhead; the corner of 3rd and D; and the corner of 4th and D. Between these corners were some scattered buildings (which included Lewis Anker's store, James A. Brazelton's livery stable, Pine's Hotel, and a feed store), but very few.

"One corner, Third and D, was known as 'Whiskey Point.' There was a saloon where the Bear Market now stands, and one across the street where the Towne and Allison drug store now stands."

Stage line depots were on both sides of Whiskey Point, along with a cluster of saloons—all within easy reach of miners and loggers returning on the stage from the desert and mountains.

The corner was a hangout for men down on their luck, sharpies, drunks and prostitutes. It could also get down right rowdy.

"I remember well", continued Atwood, "When some of the other boys and I were playing on D Street, between Third and Fourth Streets, when we heard a noise and uproar down on corner of Third and D.

"We looked down that way and saw a lot of men running out of the saloon. They all seemed to be afraid; some of them were trying to hide around the corner. Presently a couple of men ran out into the street. They pulled their revolvers and went to shooting.

"When the smoke cleared away, two men were lying dead in the street. We boys traveled back in the opposite direction. There wasn't much excitement over the shooting, because that was a common occurrence.

"We had no city officers at that time and no city government (San Bernardino had unincorporated and disincorporated several times between 1854 and 1886). Of course we had a county sheriff. His time was spent mostly in running after horse thieves and wild Indians...He let the town take care of itself."[10]

THE EARPS SETTLE DOWN

Soon after arriving in San Bernardino, the Earps rented a farm on the Carpenter Ranch, near the Santa Ana River in what is now the city of Redlands.[11]

In a rambling and somewhat incoherent letter to his friend, James Copla, in Pella on April 2, 1865, Nick appraised their new home:

"Now for what I am doing I succeeded in renting a fine farm the 3rd day after I got to San Barnardino and on the 25th day moved out to it about 10 miles from San Barnardino it has ten acres in peach & apple ortchard & 35 in graps

Oh don't I wish you and anay others of my friends was here to help me to eat apple peaches and graps this fall and drink wine.

... This is the finest climate in the world altho I dont know that I shall stay here and I shall not fore I did not start from home expecting to stop hear when we got heare we are all so near run through that we would not go any longer...

... we can say what we please heare and none dare molest or make us afraid I have enjoyed my self here cince i have bin hear and seen more peace and freedom than I did the last three years I stayed in Iowa heare people that are Seces [favoring secession from the Union] make no boan in saying so they hollow for Jef Davis when they please

... Let me now everything that you think will be of any importance to me John Hamilton is on a farm about 5 miles from me Curtis & Rusaw (Rousseau) is in Sroader Beleave me as ever your cincear friend

(signed) N.P. Earp[12]

While living on the Carpenter Ranch, Nick Earp managed to find ample opportunities to visit downtown San Bernardino, where he became a prominent figure championing the cause of the common man against what he called the hypocrisy of big business and politicians. Nick was elected foreman of the grand jury in 1867.[13]

But farm life didn't appeal much to the Earp boys. According to Earp historian, Glenn G. Boyer, young Wyatt decided one time to run away for a few days "vacation" and the return home was greeted by a whipping from his old man.

During the fall of 1868, Nick, frustrated that nobody

stuck around long enough to help out—Jim and Morgan had gone to the mining towns of Montana while Virgil and Wyatt worked for a while with a Salt Lake-bound freight wagon and later for the Union Pacific—left the Golden State and headed back to the Midwest. Nick looked up Virgil and Wyatt, who found work at the Union Pacific railhead in Wyoming and they all made the trip back to Iowa.[14]

After selling off some property, the Earps (minus Virgil, James and Wyatt) returned to Southern California in 1877. On this second journey, the family stopped at Dodge City where Wyatt was working on the local police force.

The California bound Earps stopped in San Bernardino and Nick bid for a janitor job position in the court house, but lost out to someone else. Unable to secure any other employment in town, the family moved on to a small farming community a few miles southeast of Corona called Temescal. Nick did some farming and ran a grocery store there for the next couple years.[15]

Temescal's aggressive thinking newcomer made his presence known real fast. Nick stirred up political rivalries among its residents over issues of the proposed new California Constitution and virtues of the newly established Greenback Party. According to the press:

"In Temescal they have had a political funeral. They have actually gone through the process of a political funeral, and have raised a monument inscribed as-but go Mr. Earp and he will recite to you the inscription. Now this is cold fact.

Mr. Earp, the old man eloquent of Temescal, is in town. He informs us that Temescal is simply solid for the new Constitution—that there is not a dissenting vote. He also informs us that the people in that precinct will vote for no man opposed to the new deal of reform. That is the proper spirit."[16]

Nick Earp was an ardent follower of the Greenback Party, which was organized in 1874. The group was opposed to the retirement or reduction of greenbacks and favored their increase as the only paper currency. Nick wrote an essay (which was most likely edited) entitled "The Greenback Question", which was published on July 27, 1878:

"The issues involved in this question are engaging the attention and earnest discussion of all our people ... It is not, as has been stated, a contest against capital, but the movement is the result of the cool, deliberate reflection of men who are awakening to the fact that they have been ruled long enough by the political demogogues who make their own elevation and preferment paramount to what is of vital interest to their constituents...

The day has passed when a few cross-roads politicians can meet in convention and with stereotyped sets of resolutions shackle the honest but humble citizen, and with the party lash keep him in the ranks of the party, when his very soul revolts at the measures of men... The timid and obscure man has heretofore had no hand in the management of our public affairs ... That day has passed, and the people, 'the bone and sinew,' now assert the right to have a voice in the deliberations which so nearly concern them ...Demogogues and designing men may be among the leaders of the Greenback Party; hypocrites may wear a ministeral garb, but it detracts nothing from the party or the church. Mark our prediction, that ere long candidates for important positions will be called on to express their opinions and policy; when the indorsement of the 'party' will not be sufficient to hide their want of capacity and patriotism from the most casual and unpretending observer..."

As it turned out, Nick's Greenback Party nominees lost, but the new state constitution passed and remains in effect today.[17]

Perhaps missing the excitement of a big town, the Earps left Temescal during the latter part of 1880 and moved back to the San Bernardino area. It didn't take long for Nick to be involved in a heated (political?) altercation in one of his new hangouts. The San Bernardino Daily Times reported on October 14, 1880:

"This afternoon as Mr. Earp and several other gentlemen were conversing in Mr. Ritler's store, Mr. Baily came in and made some abusive remarks, interrupting the conversation. Mr. Ritler asked the crowd to leave his store, whereupon Mr. Baily attacked him, and left some bruises on his face. No arrests had been made at the hour of going to press."[18]

The Earps settled down in Colton, a few miles southwest of San Bernardino. They would make that town their home for quite a spell. According to early Colton pioneer, Wilson Hanna, Nick and his family had a home on 8th Street, between "I" and "J" Streets. They also lived for a while on Mt. Vernon Avenue, between 'I" Street and the Southern Pacific Railroad tracks. [19]

During the fall of 1880, Nick resurrected an old saloon and renamed it the "Gem." His establishment did quite well in spite of the little town's non-drinking "dry" as opposed to "wet" reputation.

The Colton Semi-Tropic of November 27, 1880 mentioned:

> "GEM SALOON, N.P. EARP, PROPRIETOR, Keeps on hand the best whiskey, Wines, Brandies, Gin, Rum, Porter, Beer and cigars. Fancy Cocktails, Tom and Jerry, at all times whenever called for.... Call on N.P. Earp and test his superb Tom and Jerry. He is always on hand and ready to wait on customers."[20]

The events surrounding the October 26, 1881,"Gunfight At the O.K. Corral" and its aftermath were no doubt stressful (and deadly) for all parties involved in the Tombstone fracas. It may have also struck a nerve with the Earp father during an argument in San Bernardino.

The San Bernardino Daily Index for November 27, 1881,reported:

> "A difficulty occurred in front of the Farmers

Exchange Bank this afternoon between Byron Waters and a gentleman named Earp. Earp had been quarreling with a man named Ralph, and Mr. Waters interfering, he received a torrent of abuse from the old gentleman, which he resented in a lively manner. Earp was led off somewhat damaged about the eye, and badly lamed by falling."[21]

We may never learn the reason for Nick blowing his stack. Perhaps someone said something nasty about his boys in Tombstone and Nick replied in kind.

During the 1884 Colton election, saloon owner, Nick Earp ran for justice of the peace against "dry" candidates and won. Two years later when Virgil ran for constable and won, Nick was reelected with 136 votes to 127 for his closest competitor.[22] Although Nick represented Colton's "wets", he played no favorites where the law is concerned. The San Bernardino Weekly Times reported on the October 16, 1886:

> "Judge Earp, of Colton, is doing good work in the temperance cause by imposing heavy and frequent fines on drunks in that city."[23]

A sensational court case brought Nick a little fame on May 15, 1887. The Colton Semi-Tropic reported:

> "'A Human Fiend entices little Girls and Exposes his Person'

> Yesterday afternoon, about 3 o'clock, an excited woman rushed into Judge Earp's office, and told his honor that there was a brute of a

man down near the cannery talking to some little girls, and having gathered the little ones around him, that he exposed himself in a most beastly and indecent manner. The judge hurried to the scene, and finding the beast, took him in charge until he could find officer (Virgil) Earp, who brought the villain into court.

The woman who saw the dastard at his work, testified that he indecently exposed his person and was inticing the little girls, but could not say that he had attempted any outrage. Judge Earp would have gladly sent the wretch up for life, but looking at the testimony squarely, he was compelled to fine him $20; in default in which the prisoner was sent to the county jail for twenty days.

The people of Colton will rise in their mighty anger one of these days and there will be an interesting hemp necktie party. The man gave his name as John Smith. He is an old, gray-headed dastard, and being thoroughly sober, there is no paliation for his conduct."[24]

Two weeks after his son Virgil, was elected as the first marshal of Colton, which had just incorporated as a city, Nick was appointed as city recorder by the new Board of Trustees. [25]

SAN BERNARDINO SOCIETY OF CALIFORNIA PIONEERS

San Bernardino County has a fascinating heritage.

And, although the region may not have retained as many tangible reminders of the old days as historic preservationists would like, bold attempts to preserve its past for future generations to enjoy have been going on for over a century.

In January of 1888, George W. Suttenfield, B.B. Harris, and Sidney P. Waite, inserted a notice in the Chronicle asking anyone interested in forming a society that would preserve the history of San Bernardino County to be present at the courthouse on the 21st of that month. Thirty former frontiersmen joined that day

Posing for this publicity shot in 1888 for the San Bernardino Society of California Pioneers (Pioneer Society) is one tough group of hardy frontiersmen. Pictured from left to right are: William F. Holcomb, John Brown, Jr., John Brown, Sr., George Miller and B. B. Harris. Author's Collection.

as charter members of what became known as the San Bernardino Society of California Pioneers.

The initial membership requirements were that one had to arrive in California prior to December 31, 1850 and live in San Bernardino County before April 26, 1853—the date of the county's incorporation.

Over the years, the Pioneer Society—as it was usually called—succeeded in a number of preservation efforts. They erected a pavilion in Pioneer Park, a cost-free road leading up into the mountains, and several historical monuments in the Cajon Pass. They also constructed several log cabins, one of which served as the society's headquarters until it burned down in 1973. A new Pioneer Memorial Hall was used for a while before the dwindling membership merged with the San Bernardino Historical Society in 1982.

The 74-year-old frontiersman, Nick Earp, was part of that colorful group of retired fur trappers, miners, and veterans of previous wars who became charter members in 1888.[26]

The Pioneer Society had its share of conflicts and gripes as with many fraternity groups. But for the most part, these were fun-filled meetings with singing, square dancing and picnics. Of course, a willing participant of both good and bad scenarios was Nicholas Porter Earp.

Nick's confrontational escapade occurred while holding the distinction of being the group's oldest member and therefore having the honor of holding the prestigious cane at each meeting.

One day somebody angered the short tempered old man to the point that he promptly whacked his antagonist over the noggin with the cane, breaking it in two.

Nick's lighter affair was a singing duel with Civil War Veteran, Captain Nelson G. Gill. B.B. Harris, proposed a match between the two and the Pioneer Society Minutes reported:

> "Pioneer Harris humorously suggests that Pioneers Earp and Gill shall fight a duel—the weapons to consist of three songs, the one getting the 'best in three', to be declared the better man. The said duel to take place at our basket picnic on the 9th of Sept., 1888."[27]

Pioneer Society secretary, John Brown, Jr., wrote about the unique contest:

> "The next thing on our programme was announced to be the long talked of singing contest between Judge Earp and Captain Gill for a prize—a pan of baked beans. A committee of ladies was selected to decide the contest, consisting of Grandma Morse, Grandma Hunt and Mrs. R.A. Hopkins. As a preliminary, Judge Earp asked to be allowed to remove his shirt sleeves. Captain Gill was willing to give him every advantage—he might want to take off his shirt if it would help. Earp thought he might want to fight before the match ended.

> Gill allowed the running match would begin whenever he did.

> Earp did not like the idea of singing first, for he didn't know that Gil was going to sing love

songs, and that would surely carry away the committee and the prize too.

Gill wanted to be allowed to call in the aide of his wife.

Earp wouldn't listen to any such proposition. It was not fair for a young man (57) like Gill try to get a woman to help him against an old man of 73.

With these preliminary arrangements the combat began, Earp leading off the first round with 'Erin go Bragh,' Gill countered with 'My Heart is Light,' and the round closed with no apparent advantage on either side.

In the second round Earp led off with 'The Hunters of Kentucky', a song founded on the Battle of New Orleans. As two of the committee were daughters of one of the Hunters of Kentucky, it was plainly apparent that Earp had put in a tremendous lick and first blood was awarded to him. But Gill came to the scratch smiling. He said that he had been all through the late war and had faced the cannon several times, but never in all his life had he felt so bad. He came back at his opponent with 'Excelsior' with the 'Upidee' chorus, and amid the roars of laughter it evoked the second knockdown was awarded to Gill.

For the third round Earp came to the scratch looking decidedly groggy, but he forced the fighting with the 'Indians Lament'. He had intended giving the audience 'Twenty Years Ago', but it concluded to change his tactics. Gill came to the scratch rigged up as a miner, with blankets, pick and shovel, coffee pot, frying pan, etc., and as 'Jonathan Pancakes Doolittle' sang an original song to the tune of Susannah, Don't You Cry for Me.' Another knockdown was awarded Gill.

When time was called for the fourth round, Earp came up smiling with an original poem on a Nevada pilgrim written nearly thirty years previously. That k n o c k e d out Gill. He failed to respond, but in consideration of the e x c e l l e n t work he had done in the second and third rounds the committee decided that he should have some con-

Nick and Virginia Ann Earp posing for a photo when celebrating their 50th Wedding Anniversary. Courtesy of San Bernardino Historical and Pioneer Society.

sideration, so the contest was declared a draw and the prize ordered divided between the contestants.

William F. Holcomb, who is credited with discovering gold in the San Bernardino Mountains in an area known today as "Holcomb Valley", was then deputized to announce the decision of the committee and to present the beans to Messrs. Earp and Gill, which he did eloquently and felicitously.

The two then 'shook hands across the bloody chasm' — of beans."[28]

Nick and his wife, Virginia Ann, celebrated their golden anniversary at Kelting Hall in Colton. More than 200 guests attended the grand affair. George Lord, president of the Pioneer Society, called everyone to order. Nick and Virginia Ann were escorted to the center of the room where they were seated in two rocking chairs and handed fans to keep cool. After the pioneers sang Auld Lang Syne, Lord presented Nick with a gold-headed cane inscribed with Golden Wedding, N.P. Earp — S.B. Pioneers, July 30, '90. A plethora of gifts were given to the Earps. Included were a small vial of gold dust taken from the Yuba River in 1849; two pairs of gold spectacles; a pair of gold Masonic sleeve buttons; $10 in gold to Virginia Ann for pin money from District Attorney William J. Curtis, who was a member of the Earp led wagon train from Iowa to San Bernardino in 1864 and a $5 gold piece from Holman Curtis, who was a baby during that trek. They received two envelopes from Virgil and Wyatt, each containing $40. Nick's good friend, B.B. Harris gave Virginia Ann a meerschaum pipe and told her: "Mother Earp, I present you with this pipe. It is the pipe of peace; and when you have trouble with the old man, just put it in your pipe and smoke it."[29]

When the "Pioneers" got together again at their August 9th meeting, an emotional Nick Earp told his comrades what their presence meant to him. Acting secretary, William F. Holcomb mentioned in the Society's minutes:

> "Pioneer Earp being called upon responded in a very feeling speech reiterating his highest praise and appreciation of the Pioneers who attended his golden wedding at Colton on the 30th of July, declaring that no language could express his appreciation and regard for the Pioneers who paid him and his good wife such a fraternal and pleasant visit on that occasion.

> ...he said that the golden-headed cane, being a present from the Pioneer Society, was far more highly praised than any other gift he ever received in his lifetime."[30]

Heart warming affairs like the golden wedding anniversary and get- togethers at the Pioneer Society were quite enjoyable but happy times were becoming few and far between for Nick Earp as his beloved family began dying out one by one.

Morgan was murdered in March of 1882, in retaliation from the shooting deaths of Billy Clanton and the McLaury brothers. The youngest son, Warren was killed in a saloon brawl at Willcox, Arizona in 1900.

Then Virgil died of pneumonia at Goldfield, Nevada in 1905.

After his wife Virginia's death on January 14, 1893, at the age of 72, Nick met an attractive widow by the name of Annie Cadd Alexander at one of the Society meetings later that year. There appeared to be a mutual gravitation between the old pioneer and this rather eloquent and sophisticated lady. They were married on October 14, 1893.

The Weekly Chronicle covered the ceremony and reported in its October 22 issue:[31]

> "Pioneer B.B. Harris referred to the remarkable wedding celebrated before the society last Saturday, which from the longevity of so many of the happy participants afforded a strong argument of the salubrity of California climate. The groom, Pioneer N.P. Earp, aged 80; the bride, Mrs. Alexander, 50; the best lady, who gave the bride away, Mrs. M.O. Kelting, aged 60; the best man, who gave the groom away, Col. A.J. Kelting, 82; the sisters who scattered rice on the wedding couple, aged 78, 62, and 60; those who cast the slippers, 60, 58, and 56; a large number present all the way from 60 to 80; all presided over by the venerable president of the Pioneer Society, Uncle George Lord, now in his 93rd year, was surely a gathering of people that in some of the states of our Union would begin to be regarded as advancing in years, but to see these people assembled at this wedding in the most buoyant and happy spirits, many of them tripping the light fantastic in a most easy and

graceful manner, was a sight not soon forgotten, and is the strongest proof that in California
people never grow old, and between the ages of
60 and 90 there may be found some celebrating
and participating in weddings."[32]

Perhaps the initial infatuation for each other fizzled
or that Nick and Annie simply found little in common
(there was a 30 year age difference). But the marriage
turned out to be little more than in name only as Nick
frequently left the ranch that Annie had inherited on
1900 West 7th Street in San Bernardino to stay with
daughter Adelia in Yucaipa.

In December of 1897, the old frontiersman severely
injured his left shoulder when he was thrown from a
horse and his health went steadily down hill from then
on.

Nicholas Porter Earp died in the Soldier's Home at
Sawtelle, near Los Angeles on February 12, 1907. He
was 93.[33]

END NOTES

1. Boyer, Glenn G., I Married Wyatt Earp, p. 130, 1976.
2. Edwards, Jean Whitten, *Earp Family Genealogy*, Breckenridge, Texas: Beck Printing, 1991.
3. IBID
4. Boyer, Glenn G., *Wyatt Earp: Legendary American*, (series) *True West Magazine*, 1993.
5. National Archives, Washington D.C., File WC 15-132, Examining physician's report dated January 2, 1884.
6. San Bernardino Society of California Pioneers, *Minute Book A*, April 28, 1888, p. 45.
7. Boyer, Glenn G., *Wyatt Earp: Legendary American*, (series), *True West Magazine*, 1993.
8. Rousseau, Sarah Jane, Rousseau Diary, 1864.
9. San Bernardino Public Library, Holman Curtis recollections, undated. Holman Curtis was only two years old at the time. Therefore, his recollections (in library's "Earp file" must have come from the older members of the wagon train.
10. Atwood, G.A., San Bernardino in the 1860's, reminiscing speech given to San Bernardino Lions Club in 1935, reprinted in *Odyssey*, 1979.
11. Flood, John Henry, Flood Manuscript, an unpublished biography of Wyatt Earp, edited by Earl Chafin Press, 1926.
12. Maltsberger, Elma, The Story of Colton (Letter from Nick Earp to James Copla),1974.
13. The *San Bernardino Guardian*, newspaper, November 9, 1867.
14. Boyer, Glenn G., *Wyatt Earp: Legendary American*, (series), *True West Magazine*, 1993.
15. Holladay, Fred, *The Earp Clan in San Bernardino County*, Heritage Tales, p. 22, 1978. (Holladay quotes from the *San Bernardino Daily Times* for January 1, 1878.)   Great Register of Voters for May 12, 1880 and the Temescal census for June 29, 1880, lists Nick Earp as a "farmer."
16. Holladay, Fred, *The Earp Clan in San Bernardino County*, Heritage Tales, p. 22, 1978. (Holladay quotes from the *San Bernardino Daily Times*, newspaper, April 29, 1878)
17. *San Bernardino Weekly Times*, newspaper, July 27, 1878.
18. *San Bernardino Weekly Times* (newspaper), October 16, 1880, reprinted from October 14 issue of the *Daily Times*.
19. Hanna, Wilson, written statement (undated), Colton City Li-

brary. Hanna also mentioned that he attended the second grade with Nick Earp's grandson (Adelia's son), Nicholas.

20. Chaput, Don, Earp Papers, p. 37, 1994. Chaput quotes the *Colton Semi-Tropic* (newspaper) for November 27, 1880.

21. The *San Bernardino Daily Index*, newspaper, November 27, 1881.

22. The San Bernardino County Supervisor Minutes, Book D, p. 432.

23. The *San Bernardino Weekly Times*, newspaper, October 16, 1886.

24. Holladay, Fred, *The Earp Clan in San Bernardino County*, Heritage Tales, p. 26, 1978.
Holladay quotes the May 15, 1887 issue of *The Colton Semi-Tropic*, newspaper.

25. Colton Board of Trustees, Proceedings, pp. 1-2, July 25, 1887.

26. San Bernardino Society of California Pioneers, Minute Book A, April 28, 1888, p. 45.

27. San Bernardino Society of California Pioneers, *Minute Book A*, April 28, 1888, p. 101.

28. San Bernardino Society of California Pioneers, *Minute Book A*, April 28, 1888, pp. 111--113.

29. Holladay, Fred, *The Earp Clan in San Bernardino County*, Heritage Tales, p. 33, 1978.

30. San Bernardino Society of California Pioneers, *Minute Book B*, August 2, 1890, pp. 170,172.

31. *San Bernardino Daily Courier*, newspaper, January 15, 1893.

32. Holladay, Fred, *The Earp Clan in San Bernardino County*, Heritage Tales, pp. 35-36, 1978. Holladay quotes the *Weekly Chronicle* in its October 22, 1893 issue:

33. *The San Bernardino Sun*, newspaper, February 2, 1907, p.6.

Chapter Three

THE LEADER OF THE EARP BOYS
VIRGIL WALTER EARP

A native of Hartford, Kentucky, Virgil Walter Earp was born on July 18, 1843. He and his family eventually moved to Illinois and then Iowa where his younger siblings were born. But when his parents were planning to move again in 1864—this time out west—Virgil couldn't make the trip as he was busy fighting for the Union Army during raging Civil War. It would be another year before he would rejoin his family in San Bernardino, California.

Rare photograph of Virgil Earp at age 19, taken in 1862 in Monmouth, IL by E. S. Cleveland. Virgil was saloon keeper in San Bernardino and a Constable in Colton. Photo courtesy Craig Fouts, San Diego.

Virgil was the most outgoing and best liked of the

brothers. He was also extremely fond of children, as his niece, Estelle Miller attested in this story:

"We liked our Uncle Wyatt alright, but Uncle Virge was the pick of us kids. He and (his wife) Allie were always bringing us something. They practically raised me and my sister, Helena. They wanted to adopt us, but mom said that she didn't have any kids to spare.

Virgil Walter Earp, Wyatt's older brother, who was actually Chief of Police of Tombstone when the Earp Boys and Doc Holliday went down and shot it out with the Cowboys. Photo taken in 1882. From the Boyer Collection.

We lived up along the Zanja on a ranch once when Uncle Virge and Aunt Allie came to visit us. We'd moved since the last time they'd been to town, so they didn't know except in a general way where to find us. So Virge drove his buggy up the road along the San-ta Ana River and every once in awhile he'd beller out, "Deelie!" That's what the family called mom, either that or Dee, nobody called her Adelia. Finally mom heard him comin' and went out to meet him. That trip I remember Uncle Virge and Aunt Allie took me and my sister, Helena, downtown (San Bernardino). They bought us both a pair of five dollar shoes—and five dollars was a lot of money in those days. You could hardly pay five dollars for a pair of shoes then, but I suppose we needed the shoes alright."[1]

Virgil was the acknowledged leader of the brothers and chief of police in Tombstone during the O.K. Corral fiasco. After his left elbow was nearly blown away in a retaliated shot gun ambush by members of the Clanton/McLaury gang and the ensuing assassination of Morgan, Virgil was sent back to his parent's home in Colton.[2]

The *San Diego Union* (copied from the *Colton Semi-Tropic*) reported on May 28, 1882:

> "From Mr. V.W. Earp, who is now a resident of Colton, and who, within the past three days, has received letters from his brothers, we learn that both Wyatt and Warren Earp are alive and well, and are ready, when there is a reasonable show of justice being done them, to come before the courts, and stand trial for all charges that may be brought against them. N.P. Earp and his wife, the father and mother of the Earp boys, are residents of Colton, as are also two of the boys, James and Virgil, and a quieter, more law abiding family we do not often meet, and from them we learn all that seek for themselves and brothers is simple justice."[3]

His fierce reputation as a gunman would be felt in

that town once again starting with a feud between the cities of San Bernardino and Colton.

WHEN SAN BERNARDINO AND COLTON ALMOST WENT TO WAR

For well over a century the railroad has played a prominent role in the development of Southern California and its linking with the rest of the nation. This is particularly the case with the neighboring cities of San Bernardino and Colton, where the rail industry has been a major contributor to the local economy by providing transcontinental service, local connections to many parts of Southern California, and cargo shipping centers.

The long romance between San Bernardino and Colton with the railroad started while both cities were going through burgeoning growth spurts in the 1880s, largely because of the development of the flourishing citrus industry within the surrounding valley. Opportunity-seeking land speculators, very much aware of the year round warm, dry Mediterranean-like climate at their grasp, found the perfect magnet for attracting frustrated easterners fed up with the frigid cold winters and suffocatingly humid summers back home by proposing new communities and agricultural colonies through the promotion of the valley as a land of sunshine, orange blossoms, and healthful living.

In luring the multitudes of newcomers to these young communities, San Bernardino and Colton quickly gained reputations as important railroad mec-

L. to R., John Pollard, Jerry Freeland and author, Nick Cataldo in March, 2002, standing at the site of the Battle of Crossing in Colton.

cas—reputations that still hold true today.

Over the years, the two cities have carried on a relatively friendly relationship... most of the time. However, there was a spell when mutual feelings for one another were not so wonderful. In fact, there was so much tension in the air that an all-out battle between the two cities seemed eminent.

This "war" between San Bernardino and Colton started in 1875 when the Southern Pacific Railroad decided to construct a transcontinental line from eastward from Los Angeles and eventually through the San Gorgonio Pass. The decision caused a lot of excitement in San Bernardino, which had been anxiously waiting for the arrival of a railroad since the city's founding more than 20 years earlier, as its citizens were promised that the route would pass through the area.

However, in return for this favor, the Southern Pacific demanded $100,000 worth of concessions for this privilege. Since there was no guarantee that its trains would actually go through the city limits, San Bernardino's outraged civic and commercial leaders flatly refused.

The Southern Pacific promptly bypassed San Bernardino by four miles to the south, arriving into what would eventually become the community of Colton before continuing on through the San Gorgonio Pass, to Yuma, and eventually to a connection with eastern lines.[4]

Feeling cheated, San Bernardino fought back by boycotting the Southern Pacific freight. All shipping was sent by mule train to the Anaheim landing, and then by steamers from the landing to San Francisco. Although it took about two weeks for freight to reach San Francisco from Colton over the railroad, the mule train/steamer transport turned out to be just as rapid.

Hopes of having a railroad arrive in town were raised once again in San Bernardino during the early 1880s when the California Southern started pushing its line northward from San Diego. Thanks to the persuasion of one of San Bernardino's most prominent citizens, Fred T. Perris, a railroad surveyor, the line meandered up the coast from San Diego to Oceanside, and then followed a route destined to pass through San Bernardino before connecting with the Santa Fe Railway at Waterman Junction (now known as Barstow).

By May of 1881, the new railroad was nearly

completed between Oceanside and Temescal Canyon. After a lengthy delay due to floodwater caused by the Santa Margarita River, which flows thought Temescal Canyon, the line reached Colton on August 21, 1882.

Robert W. Waterman, local resident of San Bernardino, was governor of California from 1887 until 1891. He was instrumental in establishing Patton State Hospital, for developing the Waterman Rifles and for his Waterman Silver Mine near today's city of Barstow. Courtesy of San Bernardino Public Library.

It appeared that it would be just a matter of days until the long awaited arrival of a railroad into San Bernardino as final arrangements were made with the California Southern for construction of the line to cross over the Southern Pacific tracks in Colton. However, progress came to a screeching halt when the Southern Pacific refused to allow installation of the necessary track, placing locomotives and cars continuously on its tracks at the crossing site and moving them only to allow for passage of Southern Pacific trains.

California Southern filed a lawsuit against the Southern Pacific. After a year of berating each other, California Southern won its suit demanding Southern Pacific to allow the crossing; but for over a month, the latter stubbornly refused to obey the court order.

In September, 1883, the big showdown that had been heating up was about to begin between the California Southern, backed by the citizens of San Bernardino, and the Southern Pacific, supported by the Colton people.[5]

VIRGIL: SPECIAL AGENT FOR THE SOUTHERN PACIFIC

Virgil Earp was hired by the Southern Pacific as a special agent to protect its interest in the crossing fight. Although still convalescing a shoulder wound from a shotgun blast in Tombstone after the frenzied encounter with the Clantons and McLaurys near the O.K. Corral in Tombstone two years earlier, Earp was believed to still be able to handle a gun well enough to match his fierce reputation as a "dead shot." Feelings among the residents of both San Bernardino and Colton regarding the issue of the crossing ran high. Arguments leading to fist fights were becoming frequent.

The boiling point was finally reached when the two sides lined up at the crossing geared up for a brutal battle.

The infuriated San Bernardino people, determined to see the completed rail crossing— by force if necessary—lined up on the north side of the tracks, while a group of several hundred irritated Colton residents stood just south of the Southern Pacific main line.

Virgil, heavily armed, was stationed inside the cab of a locomotive which blocked the crossing.

The opposing crowds were armed with picks, shovels, shotguns, pistols and anything else that they could get a hold of. One false move would result in a bloody riot.[6]

According to eyewitness, Seth Hartley, while the angry crowds were facing off, a short session was held between future governor, Robert W. Waterman, and Sheriff Burkhart in the San Bernardino County Court House. Then a posse of experienced gunmen was quickly deputized and headed for Colton.

Waterman's party formed the spearhead of the San Bernardino forces about to clash with the Colton enemy. As Waterman, the sheriff, and the posse rode up, cheers arose from the San Bernardino people.

A short distance from the engine, the sheriff read the court order to Virgil demanding that he have the engine removed. If Virgil refused and even showed the slightest motion toward his gun, he was ordered to be shot down.

No doubt nervously reminiscing about his near fatal plight into eternity in Tombstone, Virgil knew that he may not be so lucky this time and wisely obeyed the court order and laid down his gun.

As the elated San Bernardino and frustrated Colton crowds went their separate ways, the engine was quickly taken and the crossing was installed.

On September 13, 1883, the first California Southern train—soon to be taken over by the Santa Fe Railway—rolled across the Southern Pacific tracks from San Diego and arrived in San Bernardino with the long anticipated shouts of joy and blowing of whistles.[7]

COLTON'S FIRST MARSHAL

In 1886 Virgil served a short stint as the young town's constable, beating his opposition by 137 votes to 23. His useless left arm didn't seem to lessen his efficiency or ability as a peace officer. Virgil's sister Adelia recalled an incident in Colton in 1887, when a few staggering young drunks made an uncomplimentary remark about his crippled left arm:

> "In about a tick of the clock, he (the drunk) was off his feet, right up off the street and onto the sidewalk, and pretty hard against the wall, spread-eagled. Virgil did all this in one move, with one arm. He sure was a strong feller! He just frisked this young drunk a bit rough and pushed him away, and said "Now you just run along home, boy."[8] [This testimony to Virgil's' tough exterior was quoted from the unpublished memoirs of Adelia Earp Edwards which are on file at the city library, in Colton, California. It is important to note here that some historians insist that these memoirs are fictitiously made up by David H. Cruickshanks, who is credited for transcribing them. Despite some historian's apprehensions on this matter, I personally can-

not understand why someone (Cruickshanks) would put in so much work without any monetary gain. [As an objective historian, I must look at all information purported to be accurate and make them available for the reader.]

Obviously quite pleased with their firm, no-nonsense constable, Colton's citizens voted Virgil Earp for a nine month term as the newly incorporated city's first marshal in July, 1887.

Other than dealing with occasional petty thieves, slobbering drunks, wife beaters, opium smokers, and check forgers, his daily routine in Colton hardly measured up to the common "Wild West" misconception of facing down badmen and trailing cattle rustlers on a twenty-four hour basis. Instead, Virgil's responsibilities resembled more of what Andy and Barney dealt with in the old 1960s sitcom, "Andy Griffith Show". The following anecdotes from minutes of various Colton Board of Trustees meetings attest to this:

"Bill submitted by V.W. Earp to Trustees for 75 cents for lock and key for jail."

"Bill submitted by V.W. Earp to Trustees for $4.25 for cost of nails and meals for prisoners."

"Bill submitted to Trustees for $20.00 for sewer work performed by Marshal V.W. Earp."[9]

During his free time Virgil would occasionally ride out through the Cajon Pass and on to Lone Pine Canyon where his good friend, Almon Clyde, owned a large ranch. Virgil, Almon and sometimes Wyatt would hunt deer in the area.

Virgil loaned his hay baler to Almon Clyde and the Earp boys helped their friend out by cutting and baling hay on the property. Virgil never did take the baler home with him and the Clyde family still has it today.[10]

Don Chaput mentions in his book, *Virgil Earp: Western Peace Officer* that in the Pacific Coast Directory for

Almon Clyde's house built in Lone Pine Canyon in 1872. Still standing today, Virgil and Wyatt visited there often. Photo taken in 1994. Author's Collection.

1886-87, Virgil was listed as proprietor of the Bijou Theater at 78 Third Street in San Bernardino in addition to his work as a peace officer.

Virgil was easily reelected as marshal of Colton in April of 1888, for a two year term while his father, Nick

Earp was reappointed city recorder.

Don Chaput also noted in *Virgil Earp: Western Peace Officer,* that Virgil tried to get the Republican nomination for sheriff of San Bernardino County in July of that

Virgil Earp's home (still standing) at 528 H. St. in Colton. Author's Collection.

year. Unfortunately, he lost out to E.C. Seymour of San Bernardino who was elected sheriff in the November election.[11]

The marshal's job brought a decent income for Virgil, and while in that position he purchased a new home in Colton, at 528 W. "H" Street. The following entry, dated July 7, 1888, is taken from the county register of deeds book. It is also a testimony to the close relationship he had with his wife Allie:

"I, Virgil Earp, of the city of Colton, County of San Bernardino, and state of California, for and in consideration of the love and affection which I bear towards my wife, and as an expression of my heartfelt gratitude to her for her constant, patient and heroic attendance at my bedside while I lay dangerously wounded at Tombstone, Arizona, grant unto my wife, Mrs. Alvira Earp, as her separate estate, all that real property situated in the city of Colton...[Lots 5 and 6, Block 113]

... Witness my hand this 7th day of July 1888.

Virgil W. Earp (Signed)[12]

On March 9, 1889, Virgil Earp retired as Colton's City Marshal with 13 months left of his two-year term. According to the minutes of the Colton City Board of Trustees, Virgil resigned under pressure for neglecting his duties. It is unclear why he resigned rather than simply attend to his lawman duties. Most likely, he grew tired of the job and was itching to move on to new adventures.[13]

Sure enough, Virgil found a new interest when he refereed the first "legal" prize fight held in San Bernardino on December 24, 1889. In that match, Jack Sullivan beat Joe Cotton in the 32nd round. According to the *San Bernardino Weekly Courier*:

"For our part, we think there is more demoralization in a bar-room row, or a street brawl, than there is in a hundred such boxing matches as that of Tuesday night.

To commence with, boys were not admitted to the Opera House. There was no vulgar black-guardism, no obscenity, no profanity, no brutality characterizing the proceedings...

The management of the affair, by Virgil Earp, was perfect. Absolutely fair play was insisted upon. No outside interference was permitted. The men knew that they were there to fight, and not to fake—to box with gloves, not to engage in brutal slugging, or savage rough and tumble...

Whether this is but the beginning of pugilistic (sic) sport in San Bernardino we do not know, but we know that if it is, and such affairs can be conducted as they were...even the most rigid moralist can have little fault to find with them. Should there be any attempt made in the future to introduce degrading features into boxing matches, it will not take San Bernardino long to suppress all such exhibitions, but that any such attempt will be made, while Virgil Earp is the manager of such affairs, is impossible."[14]

In 1890, Virgil opened a gambling hall in San Bernardino on the north side of 3rd Street, between "D" and "E" Streets. It was located on the second floor inside the Saterwhite Building, above what later became the Isis Theater.

Former county clerk, Harry L. Allison, was interviewed by the *San Bernardino Sun* in April, 1957 and described the Earp brothers as being "very affectionate" toward each other. While working as a messenger boy for the Postal Telegraph Company, Allison often took telegrams to Virgil and the gamblers in his second story hall which included card tables, dice games, roulette wheel, etc., but had no bar. Allison recalled:

> "Virgil was a gentleman...he had me take off my hat and hold up the message whenever I entered."

> "Young man, who do you want to see?" he'd ask. I'd give him the name and he would direct me to the man. I was the only kid allowed in there. He always taught me to say, 'Yes, sir', or 'No, sir.' "Allison also revealed a sound piece of advice that Earp frequently gave him..."Young man, you never win at gambling!"

> Virgil also made sure that the lad got a good tip for delivering the messages too. "Many times the gamblers would give gold, and if it was small, he'd toss me a blue chip", said Allison.

Another man who was well aquatinted with the Earp boys was O.J. Fisk, who arrived in San Bernardino County in 1892, about the time Virgil was running a cigar store in the St. Charles Hotel.[15]

He saw Wyatt a number of times whom he described as:

> "Quiet and wouldn't talk much about himself. But, yes, he was a cheerful agreeable man. In appearance, to me, he even looked kind of studious, but he always took part in the dances and get togethers they had in those days."

Fisk knew Virgil best of all though as both men took part in the gold strike out in the Mojave Desert's New York Mountains and helped form the mining town of Vanderbilt.[16]

The *San Bernardino Times-Index* for April 28, 1893, announced that Virgil Earp arrived in Vanderbilt with a wagon load of lumber and gambling equipment. When Fisk arrived in Vanderbilt, Virgil was running "Earp's Hall", a two story saloon with a public hall upstairs.[17]

"I was about 19 years old at the time...Those days there wasn't much to do but hang out around the saloon in those towns when you weren't working. I got to know Virgil pretty well.

"He was a pretty nice, gentlemanly sort of fellow, I liked him very much."

Vanderbilt was a busy place where there was always something going on. On the second floor of Earp's Hall, attractions ranged from dances and prize fights to church on Sundays. Fisk recalled:

"The new camp's name expressed the high hopes of everyone who lived there. 'Vanderbilt' meant enormous wealth...We all believed that it would be found in great quantity under those rugged mountains and so did hundreds of other people... They came on horseback, in wagons and buckboards, and with the burro trains carrying all their worldly possessions. The four-horse stage to Goffs was so crowded that 'fares' often road on the roof. One day, so many climbed on the top that it was caved in by their weight...

Vanderbilt had two stores, five saloons and a weekly newspaper, The *Vanderbilt Shaft*. Its only two story building was a saloon owned by Virgil Earp...The second floor was a dance hall, where many a night I danced to the strains of an orchestra consisting of a small organ operated by foot-pedals and one fiddle. Virgil had one arm badly crippled during a fun-fight at Tombstone, but he managed to do this bartending with the other. Two of his professional gamblers were notorious characters known to everybody as High Pockets and Blood Alley Mose. They kept miners busy at the poker tables after pay day, and were excellent hands at separating them from their cash...

There was a lot of playful shooting at different times all in a spirit of clean fun. I was attending a dance at Earp's Hall when a miner staggered into the room and began to throw lead. His target was the organ that furnished us with our dance music. Several bullets found their mark. Naturally the boys were furious. They swarmed around the intruder and hustled him out of the building. We had no jail in Vanderbilt, so they locked him up in a tunnel that was fitted with a door and used as a powder magazine. Within an hour, the prisoner had pried loose the wedges...and returned to the dance. Meanwhile we discovered that none of the organ's vital parts had been damaged by his fusillade, so he was forgiven and allowed to stay after he promised to be good."[18]

Virgil and Allie returned to Colton in 1904. The city trustees there had recently voted to grant one new saloon license, which would have increased the number of saloons in town from one to two. Virgil decided to apply for that new license on June 29 but on July 6, the city Board of trustees minutes reported that he lost out to J.A. Teutschman.[19]

An Earp family reunion took place shortly after a new gold strike broke out in Nevada. Adelia Earp described the occasion in her memoirs as follows:

> "We all had a big meeting here about thirty years back (1903) at the hotel of a friend, Mr. Billicke. There was Mr. Billicke, Wyatt and Josephine, Virgil and Allie, and Jim. The boys were about ready to go back to Goldfield, Nevada, where they had mining claims. I recall they asked us to go with them but of course we could not go out there then. ... We had a great comfortable green room, with big comfortable green furniture, and I well recall how Virge and Wyatt sat together on a green ottoman and stretched those long legs along that thick green carpet ... Virgil said to me, booming like he did all of a sudden, 'Deelie pour some coffee now, and put some of that there whiskey in.' We all had a real fine time. I recall how the boys talked of (President Theodore) Roosevelt, especially Jim. ... Later Mr. Billicke brought my father. He was very old and very ill then ... these are the things I like to recall now. Later Wyatt took us to the hotel of a lady and Bill (Adelia's husband) and I had a fine time."[20]

Virgil and his wife, Allie, took part in the excitement. While still holding on to their Colton home, they headed for the new mining camp of Goldfield during the middle of 1904.

On January 26, 1905, Virgil was sworn in as deputy sheriff of Esmeralda County by Sheriff J.F. Bradley with the specific assignment of working in Goldfield. He also became the Special Officer for a popular watering hole called the National Club, where he served as a bouncer.[21]

The late San Bernardino County historian, Fred Holladay, who did extensive research on the Earp family, mentioned in an article published in the Nevada Official Bicentennial Book entitled *The Earp Brothers in Goldfield*:

> "In February 1905, promoter Tex Rickard opened the *Northern*, Goldfield's most celebrated saloon and gambling house, in a building adjoining the National Club. Wyatt, who had met and become friends with Tex in Nome, Alaska, was hired to be one of his pit bosses, overseeing the club's gaming tables.
>
> Rickard's Northern boasted a 50-foot-long bar, dispensing six barrels of whiskey daily. It became great fun for habituate to greet the great gunfighter Wyatt Earp at Rickard's saloon and then drift next door to have a drink with his brother Virgil.
>
> However, only a short time later, Virgil came down with a bad cold which developed into pneumonia. On the critical list for several days, he finally recovered and resumed work at the

National.

Then, on July 8, 1905, Goldfield suffered its first major fire when a stove exploded in the Bon Ton Millinery Shop. The flames soon spread to adjoining structures as volunteer firemen and hundreds of town residents rushed to the scene. Virgil, as deputy sheriff, was undoubtedly on the fire line.

Goldfield was saved when the wind shifted to the southeast, but not before two blocks of business houses burned to the ground."[22]

Virgil was still wearing the badge in Goldfield when he was stricken with pneumonia three months later. This time he couldn't make it back and died on October 19, 1905, at the age of 62. At the request of his daughter, Jane, born during his first marriage, Virgil Earp was buried in Riverview Cemetery in Portland, Oregon.[23]

END NOTES

1. Boyer, Glenn G., unpublished manuscript, Colton Public Library, pp. 12-13.

2. Boyer, Glenn G., *I Married Wyatt Earp*, p. 37, 1976.

3. Chaput, Don, *The Earp Papers*, p. 125, 1994.

4. Ingersoll, L.A., *Century Annals of San Bernardino County 1769 to 1904*, pp. 253-255, 1904.

5. IBID, pp. 257-260.

6. *Riverside Press and Horticulturist* (newspaper), August 11, 1883.

7. Hartley, Seth, "War Between Colton and San Bernardino..." *Colton Courier*, June 1, 1939.

8. Edwards, Adelia, Memoirs, p. 11, written in 1932-1934, copyright, David H. Cruickshanks, 1978.

9. Turner, Alford E. and Oster, William W., *Colton's Marshal Earp*, Colton Public Library.

10. Clyde, Robert, Oral interview with author, 1990.

11. Chaput, Don, *Virgil Earp: Western Peace Officer*, p. 178, 1994.

12. Land Deed (copy) for Virgil Earp, San Bernardino's Norman Feldheym Central Library, July 7, 1888.

13. Sheffield, Larry, "Why Did Virgil Earp Resign?" *San Bernardino Sun*, p. B7, August 7, 2005. I also had correspondences with Dr. Sheffield about the matter in June of 2004.

14. Holladay, Fred, "The Earp Clan in San Bernardino County", *Heritage Tales*, p. 30, 1978.

15. *San Bernardino Weekly Times*, p.7, September 30, 1892.

16. Saulsbury, James M., "Famed Earp Family Well-Known in San Bernardino Area", *San Bernardino Sun*, April 17, 1957.

17. *San Bernardino Times-Index*, April 28, 1893.

18. Fisk, O.J., as told to Philip Johnston, "Treasures From Vanderbilt," *Westways*, June, 1952.

19. Sheffield, Larry, "Why Did Virgil Earp Resign?" *San Bernardino Sun*, p. B7, August 7, 2005.
I also had correspondences with Dr. Sheffield about the matter in March of 2006.

20. Edwards, Adelia, Memoirs, pp. 13-14, written in 1932-1934, copyright, David H. Cruickshanks, 1978.
Adelia did not mention what city the reunion was in. It may have occurred in San Bernardino, but more than likely in Los Angeles as Nick was moved into the nearby soldier's home at Sawtelle sometime in 1903.

21. State of Nevada, County of Esmeralda, Oath of Office, signed June 26, San Bernardino's Norman Feldheym Central Library 1905.

22. Holladay, Fred, *The Earp Brothers in Goldfield*, in Nevada Official Bicentennial Book, Edited by Stanley W. Paher, Las Vegas: Nevada Publications, 1976, pp. 319--320.

23. *The Oregonian* (newspaper) for April 22, 1899, mentions about Virgil's reunion with his daughter. Obituary from the *Oregonian* (newspaper), October 24, 1905. Official death records, Riverview Cemetery Association, Portland, Oregon, October 25, 1905.

Chapter Four

LONG MAY HIS STORY BE TOLD
WYATT BERRY STAPP EARP

He spent more of his life in Southern California's San Bernardino County than anywhere else. But if the man had to depend on his exploits here to justify his claim to fame, he'd be remembered primarily as a citizen who preferred the solitude of the desert—quite a contrast to his highly magnified reputation attained in the bustling gambling halls and saloons of Kansas and Arizona.

The fact is, Wyatt Earp, whose name has been immortalized for his ex-

Wyatt Earp at 38-years-old from the author's collection.

ploits in Tombstone and other wild camps, spent five times as much of his life as a mine developer in San Bernardino County than he did as a frontier lawman.

Plans for moving Wyatt and his family out to this area from their home in Pella, Iowa, began shortly after brother Jim's discharge from active duty as a union soldier in the Civil War due to a severely wounded shoulder suffered in 1863.[1]

While two other brothers, Newton and Virgil, were still fighting in the raging conflict, Wyatt's father, Nick, quit his job as assistant provost marshal and pulled up stakes for a move out to a beautiful Southern California valley that he briefly passed through on his way home from prospecting back in 1851. This valley, so impressive with its fertile fields, boundless timber lands, and deep, clear water streams, was called San Bernardino.[2]

In 1864, Nick Earp organized a wagon train made up of three other Pella families: the Rousseaus, the Hamiltons, and the Curtises. And on May 12, 1864, they embarked for the trip out west.

According to Jesse Curtis, great-grandson of one party member, the train started out with 30 people, including Wyatt, his parents, older brother, Jim and younger siblings, Morgan, Warren, and Adelia. Three children were born to the other families later on during the journey.

Mrs. Sarah Jane Rousseau, who kept a diary of the trip, mentioned that after they made their first night's camp, seven more wagons straggled in late. By the time the caravan reached its destination there were about a dozen wagons in all.[3]

During the arduous journey across the barren plains, the desolate Mojave Desert, and through the rugged Cajon Pass, Nick and Jim did most of the driving. Meanwhile the 16-year-old Wyatt spent much of the time doing necessary chores such as fetching water and food, babysitting his 3-year-old sister, Adelia, and occasionally helping out by driving a wagon.

The wagon train reached San Bernardino on December 17, 1864. According to Holman Curtis, one of the young children in the party, the families set up camp in San Bernardino just east of what is today Sierra Way and Court Street.[4] Soon afterward, the Earps rented a farm a few miles east on the Carpenter Ranch near the Santa Ana River in what is now the city of Redlands.

In his unpublished biography of Wyatt Earp, long time friend, John H. Flood Jr., described the Earps' first Christmas meal in their new home.

> "Around a table loaded with the fruits and sweetmeats of a northern clime, a family of five children (James, Virgil, Wyatt, Morgan and Adelia) and a father (Nicholas) and mother (Virginia Ann) were seated at a feast of glorious thanksgiving in the little village of San Bernardino on the Christmas Day of Eighteen and Sixty-four. There were evidences of their having come recently through an ordeal."[5]

Earp historian Glenn Boyer recalled in his *True West* biography (1993), an interview he had with Estelle Miller, daughter of Adelia. Mrs. Miller told him that shortly after arriving in San Bernardino, young Wyatt made it well known that he wasn't cut out to be a farmer. In fact, one day he decided to run away for a few days "vacation" only to return home for a whipping from his old man who proceeded to kick him off the farm.[6]

Information on Wyatt during the next few years is somewhat sketchy and much of it comes from Stuart N. Lake's often questioned biography, *Wyatt Earp: Frontier Marshal*. Lake corresponded with Wyatt several times during the late 1920s with the purpose of writing an accurate biography. But when *Frontier Marshal* came out in 1931—two years after his death in 1929—Wyatt came out looking like a knight on a white horse combating enemies of law and order. This "paladin" image inspired numerous movies, a television show—and ultimately, the Wyatt Earp legend.

According to Lake's book, at the age of 17, Wyatt began driving stage coaches for General Phineas Banning between Los Angeles and San Bernardino during the summer of 1865 as an emergency replacement for Banning's regular driver, who had broken his leg. Then, during the winter of 1865-1866, he drove freight wagons for Frank Binkley from the port of San Pedro, California, through San Bernardino, across the desert, past the Salton Sea, the Colorado River and on to Prescott, Arizona.[7]

Lake recorded more Wyatt Earp "heroics"—which may or may not be true. One portrays Wyatt driving a 16 animal freighting outfit for Chris Taylor between San Bernardino and Salt Lake City, Utah, during the spring of 1866. The author wrote:

"The Salt Lake trace traversed seven hundred miles of the most difficult desert and mountain wilderness, through a territory infested by the Paiutes."

Lake also notes that when Wyatt returned from the Salt Lake trek, he was chosen as one of a select group of freighters by San Bernardino County Sheriff, John King, to go on a rescue of a small detachment of U.S. soldiers surrounded and trapped by several hundred Paiute Indians in the Mojave Desert at Camp Cadiz.

No research has proven that a "Camp Cadiz" ever existed. However, noted Mojave Desert historian, Dennis G. Casebier, came up with something interesting when he wrote a small booklet in 1972 entitled The Battle of Camp Cady. He mentioned that the army camp, which was located on the banks of the Mojave River, was involved in a skirmish between soldiers and Indians on June 29, 1866. On that day, Second Lieutenant James R. Hardenbergh, who was in charge of Camp Cady, led a platoon of six men in an attack on a band of Paiutes who were passing by. The soldiers were no match for the Indians who—by the lieutenant's estimation was 36 in number—and were soundly beaten. Three of his men were killed and at the conclusion of the fight, there were only eight men left at the fort— Hardenbergh, the camp doctor, a sergeant and three privates.

Hardenbergh thought for sure that he and his surviving men would be annihilated. Help was coming from the army and even a company of civilians from San Bernardino was put together but the Paiutes had no intention of keeping the fight going.

It is possible that Wyatt was involved somehow in the anticipated retaliation effort at Camp "Cady" and Lake's Camp "Cadiz" may have simply been a misspelling.

In any event, the Paiutes had no intention of keeping the fighting going. They were not the aggressors during this incident and a battle with the troupes were not in their plans. They had fought an unwanted battle.[8]

The controversial Stuart Lake notes in *Frontier Marshal* that Wyatt went into partnership with Charles Chrisman in the spring of 1867, hauling freight to Salt Lake City. In the Flood Manuscript, this information is also given.[9]

Glenn Boyer, though, states in his *True West* biography of Wyatt Earp, that it was older brother Virgil who did the actual driving while the younger Wyatt did menial work for the freighters as a "swamper".[10]

Lee A. Silva, author of the epic *Wyatt Earp--A biography of the Legend: Vol. 1, The Cowtown Years* (2002), clearly mentions that there was an early San Bernardino pioneer during that time by the name of Charles "Crisman". Silva's contention is that Wyatt obviously knew about Crisman, aware of the time and places he was talking about, and the misspelling by Lake was a phonetical error. Therefore, Wyatt's involvement with Crisman was probably true although he may not have been actually a "partner" with Crisman.[11]

Adelia Earp Edwards, recalled in her memoirs about Virgil and Wyatt working together in 1866 and 67. She also noted that Wyatt had a bit of a time holding his liquor.

"When Virgil finished stage driving he and Wyatt went to Prescott, working for a big San Bernardino freight company with great wagons and long teams of mules and oxen. When they arrived in Prescott, all the men went to a saloon in town to celebrate a mite. Wyatt had hardly taken a drink before and the whiskey soon had him reeling. Real drunk! He just passed on out and Virgil and another friend took him off to his bed. When he woke up, he was in a terrible state alright, sick, headache, perspiring and trembling all over. Virge told him the only cure was to take a few more drinks. He did just that, and got just as bad as before. By the time he was close to sobering up, it was time for that rough old return journey and he suffered so bad for a day or two he swore not to touch whiskey again. And he kept to that for twenty years! But he would take a couple glasses of beer or wine most days, but that was about all."[12]

Virgil and Wyatt later worked for the Union Pacific Railroad, which was building west. Both brothers started out as shovel men, but eventually Virgil worked as a teamster and while Wyatt continued as a pick and shovel man.

In the fall of 1868, Nick Earp, frustrated that none of the boys were home to help out on the farm (Jim had gone to the mining towns of Montana, taking young

Morgan with him), left California and headed back to the Mid West by wagon and then caught a train at the Union Pacific railhead in Wyoming. Somewhat cooled off by now, he looked up his boys near the railhead, and they all made the trip back to the Midwest.[13]

The elder Earps moved back to their Iowa farm. A year later the family went on to Lamar, Missouri, where Nick had owned some land. They stayed there until 1877, before returning to the San Bernardino Valley with the two youngest children, Warren and Adelia.

On the return trip to Southern California, the Earps stopped in Temescal for a couple years, before moving back to the San Bernardino Valley in 1880. Settling down in Colton, Nick became the town's justice of the peace. Meanwhile, Wyatt and Jim had moved on to the Kansas cow towns of Wichita and Dodge City, the latter where Wyatt worked as an assistant marshal and Jim worked as a bartender.[14]

In 1879, Virgil, who was serving as U.S. Deputy Marshal for the Arizona Territory, contacted Jim and Wyatt in Dodge City about the new silver mining town of Tombstone and the golden opportunities that could surface there. Before long, Jim and Wyatt were on their way from Kansas while Morgan left the family home in California to join them.

Soon after arriving in Tombstone, the Earp boys filed on several mining claims. Jim began working at Vogan's Bowling Alley and stayed there until he got a job as a bartender at the newly opened Sampling Room. Wyatt immediately gained an interest in some gambling layouts while also working as a shotgun messenger for Wells Fargo, a job that Morgan eventually took over when Wyatt was appointed as Pima County Deputy Sheriff. Two years after their arrival in Tombstone, three of the brothers had their celebrated shootout with the Clantons and the McLaurys.[15]

Following the "O. K. Corral" gunfight, there was the murder of Morgan, a nearly fatal ambush of Virgil, and the retaliated killings of members of the cowboy gang. And after the return of Morgan's body to his parents' home in Colton accompanied by the grievously wounded Virgil and the brothers' wives, the surviving Earps left Tombstone for good the following year.

By February of 1884, Wyatt and Jim turned up in the gold fields of Shoshone County, Idaho, during what has become known as the "Coeur d'Alene Rush". The brothers formed a mining syndicate with Dan Ferguson and three other men—a group that was eventually sued on at least three occasions for either claim jumping or possession of land by force. Twice they received unfavorable judgments.

Later in 1884, Wyatt and Jim moved on to Eagle City and quickly recorded one of the six nearby mining claims. They opened the White Elephant Saloon in town. This venture apparently prospered until September of that year, when both Earp brothers abruptly disappeared from the scene.[16]

During the next few years, Virgil, despite his permanently damaged left arm, served as constable and later as the first city marshal in Colton. Meanwhile, Nick continued as the city's justice of the peace and Jim opened up the Club Exchange Saloon in San Bernardino with a man named J.H. Anderson. Warren, a self-proclaimed "capitalist", was living at the King House in San Bernardino.[17]

As for Wyatt, he lived in Colorado for a little while before moving back to Southern California in either 1885 or 1886. Settling down in San Diego with him was a beautiful woman "stolen" from old Tombstone adversary, Sheriff Johnny Behan. Wyatt severed a relationship with common-law wife, Celia Ann "Mattie" Blaylock, sent her back to Colton after the O.K. Corral gunfight and aftermath, and never saw her again. The new woman in Wyatt's life was Josephine Sarah "Sadie" Marcus. She would become the love of his life and steady companion until the day he died.

When the Earps arrived in San Diego, the small seacoast town of about 5,000 people was just waking up as the long awaited railroad finally arrived. Houses, commercial buildings, saloons and other structures sprang up and San Diego's population leaped to more than 26,000 by the end of 1886.[18]

During his years in San Diego, Wyatt dabbled in various real estate and business ventures and occasionally refereed boxing matches. He profited most of all from saloons and gambling halls. Kenneth R. Cilch, Sr., notes in his book, *Wyatt Earp: The Missing Years*, that Wyatt owned or leased at least four establishments, the most famous being the Oyster Bar.[19]

Wyatt and Sadie didn't own a home in San Diego. At first, they lived with Virgil (who encouraged him to move out there) and his wife Allie. But when his brother and sister-in-law moved back to Colton to be closer to his aging parents, Wyatt and Sadie had to look for other places to stay.[20]

Josephine "Sadie" Earp, c. 1880. Copy of a photo in the possession of Carmelita May- hew (photographer unknown). According to Carmelita this photo was copied extensively after the death of Johnny Behan for whom it was made. Boyer Collection.

One of their favorite accommodations was at the re- cently built Brooklyn Hotel. Referred to as a "Cowboy Victorian", it was a modest looking three story work-

The Horton Grand Hotel in San Diego in the 1980s.

ingman's hotel with 32 rooms on the upper two floors, two baths—one for women and one for men and a New England style restaurant on the bottom floor.

The Brooklyn (renamed the Kahle Saddlery in 1912) and a more attractive "Baroque revival style" edifice known as the Horton Grand Hotel, were both dismantled a century later, moved several blocks away from their original sites (across from the Horton Plaza) and rebuilt brick by brick in 1986. Today the beautifully reconstructed Horton Grand Saddlery Hotel is a luxurious 110 room hotel and restaurant complex.[21]

Always ready to try something new, Wyatt, who was listed in the San Diego City Directory for 1889 as a "Capitalist", bought several race horses with a man named E.B. Gifford and hit the California circuit—San Francisco, Santa Rosa, Napa, Exposition Park in Los

Angeles and Santa Ana. He held on to his San Diego investments for a few more years and then sold everything during the mid-1890s.[22]

Wyatt and Sadie left for San Francisco during the early 1890s and considered that city one of their favorite. The newspapers acknowledged Wyatt's tough reputation from his Tombstone days while at the same time noting his preference for sipping lemonade to guzzling booze.[23]

No matter where Wyatt was living at the time, he made it a point to spend time with his family in the San Bernardino area. Many of those visits involved Adelia's kids.

Although never fathering children Wyatt was very fond of them. However, his quiet and deliberate demeanor combined with his steely blue eyes (traits that were undoubtedly considered to be attributes when confronting adversaries) nevertheless sometimes left the young ones a bit wary of him.

A prime example of this dilemma was a story relayed by Adelia's granddaughter, Nathalie Daggett, to genealogist Marsha Patrick in 1993. Mrs. Daggett's mother told her of the time when Adelia was living in Mentone (a small community northeast of San Bernardino) and Wyatt brought a big bag of candy for the kids. However, he had to leave it in the middle of the floor because the little ones were afraid of his piercing eyes.[24]

During those family visits, it was not uncommon for Wyatt and Virgil, whose H Street home in Colton was just a short distance from their parents' residence, to ride through the Cajon Pass and on to Lone Pine Canyon where good friend, Almon Clyde, owned a large ranch. The brothers would often stay a couple weeks at a time while all three of them hunted deer during the day. The Earp brothers also helped their friend out by cutting and baling hay on the property.[25]

Wyatt's sister, Adelia Earp Edwards, spoke fondly of her big brother's visits to the San Bernardino area:

"One time when they were building the Yuma bridge (across the Colorado River), Wyatt was staying at our home for a while. This must have been about 1912. There was a big race on between a man from San Diego and a man from Los Angeles over this. The winner would get his town to have the road built through from the bridge to the coast. So it was quite an important event and all the men were placing bets. Wyatt put about all his ready cash on the man from San Diego who he knew (Col. Ed Fletcher). After a real rough and tumble race the San Diego man won, and Wyatt won a quite a deal of money.

He bought us all clothes, and toys for the youngsters, and he still had a mighty roll left for himself. He was always generous and he just loved to give presents. And he treasured presents given him. I recall his face lighting up like a little boy one time when I gave him a matching pocket book and pouch for his tobacco. And he loved books. Bill (Adelia's husband) gave him the *Virginian* [written in 1902 by Owen Wister, prototype story about the west, had a 10 year stage run, made into several motion pictures and became a television series 1962-1971] one time he stayed with us, and after that he always searched out a new book for Wyatt to read when he knew he was coming."[26]

An adventurer and opportunist, Wyatt spent much of his life roaming from boomtown to boomtown throughout the west in search of fortune. Sometimes lawman, sometimes gambler, town lot speculator, prospector, and undercover agent—he ventured into almost anything that might turn a profit.

The fact that Wyatt liked to gamble was no secret and several times in his life he amassed sizeable fortunes. He and Sadie returned to California from the Klondike gold fields in Alaska late in 1901 with $80,000 in his pocket, a large portion of which resulted from the sale of the Dexter Saloon that he ran in Nome. But with Wyatt's generosity in lending money to friends and his penchant for gambling, his money never lasted long.[27]

While visiting his family in the San Bernardino area soon after returning from Alaska in 1901, Wyatt and Virgil applied for a gambling hall permit in Colton but were turned down. With their father's retirement of several years, the little influence that the Earps once had in town was gone now.[28]

In 1902 they detoured to Tonapah where Wyatt opened the Northern Saloon, did some prospecting, and served briefly as a deputy U. S. marshal of Nye County. After an Earp family reunion in San Bernardino, both Wyatt and Virgil, along with their wives, went on to Goldfield in 1904 for a new mining venture. Virgil died there year later from pneumonia.[29]

After a life time's worth of adventures that saw him work as a buffalo hunter, gambler, officer of the law, and prospector in the Klondike gold fields, 57 year old Wyatt now decided to fulfill a longing to get away from it all. Shortly after Virgil's death in 1905, Wyatt and Sadie went to Los Angeles and prepared a return trip to the southeastern corner of the Mojave Desert, where they'd intended to roam before they were sidetracked to the Yukon. This part of the Mojave Desert they were heading for was as remote a place as anyone could find in the West. The nearest railroad was the Santa Fe line at Needles. Occasional steamboats ran between Yuma and Needles, but business was slow and the boats didn't maintain frequent schedules any more. The only mail service was a weekly mule back route between Parker and Topock. It took the rider two days each way to make the trip, and he spent the remaining three of each week recuperating. Freight and supplies could be obtained only by a 65-mile wagon trip to Needles or by an indefinite wait at one of the many little river landings. During both low water and flood periods, the river service was a real problem. This somewhat foreboded area, however, was just perfect for the Earps.[30]

During the spring of 1905 Wyatt and Sadie discovered their beloved gold and copper "Happy Days" Mines. The initial seven claims—"Copper Accident", "Colorado", "Cave", "Giant", "Hercules", "Happy Day", and "Lucky Day"—were spread out about four miles west of the Colorado River crossing at Parker, Arizo

SOUTHERN CALIFORNIA LAWMAN

Although the prospects were probably not bad, it is doubtful they ever took much paying ore from these stakes. Basically, Wyatt and Sadie wanted a place to go and meet with friends—not to make a fortune. Their mining interests (which eventually increased to nearly 100 claims) were simply an excuse to be out there. Over the next twenty years they frequently camped out next to the Happy Day Mines during the fall, winter and spring months while also maintaining a more substantial house at Vidal, about 25 miles to the southwest.

Wyatt and Sadie may have intended to get away from it all, however, the local newspaper, known as *The Needles Eye* kept tabs on seemingly every move they made.

On February 7, 1907, the paper found it noteworthy when Wyatt arrived in Needles, California "from his mines on the Colorado River".

On February 16, 1907, *The Needles Eye* mentioned about the passing of Wyatt's father, Nick Earp:

> "Wyatt Earp received the sad news Thursday (February 14th) of the death of his father, Nicholas P. Earp, at Sawtelle, California. Mr. Earp recently came up from his mining properties south of Needles and only learned upon his arrival here of the serious illness of his father. Mrs. Earp arrived in Los Angeles the first of the week and will accompany Mr. Earp to the mines in a few days."

On October 26, 1907—on the twenty-sixth anniversary of the O.K. Corral affair in Tombstone—*The Needles Eye* reported that "... Wyatt Earp, at his property on the south slope of the Whipple Mountains, has been prospecting his claim and finding satisfactory bodies of ore..."[32]

As the summer months heated up, Wyatt and Sadie lived in rented cottages in Los Angeles. And before old age could catch up with the lifelong adventurer, it was during that time of year when Wyatt got involved into some rather interesting escapades.

"Arthur M. King, a former police officer, recalled in a *True West Magazine* article in 1958 that he once served as a deputy under Wyatt Earp. Together they engaged in a series of special missions for the Los Angeles Police Department that were not "totally" within the law."

In those days it used to take two years or more to get a wanted man extradited from Mexico, so there was a steady stream of criminals south of the border", King said. So, the two lawmen would disguise themselves as miners and sneak into Mexico before bringing their man back for trial by "throwing him in irons and using a six-gun to persuade him we meant business". King described Wyatt as "a master tracker."

One such incident occurred in 1909, when the police department had a criminal by the name of Pearson that had escaped custody. A rapist and murderer, as well as a drug addict, Pearson fled the U.S. for Mexico.

Wyatt and King boarded a train and headed south for San Diego where horses were rented and supplies purchased. Once the lawmen got what they needed for the pursuit, they barely took time to sleep or eat until they found Pearson's camp.

With guns in hand, they surprised the outlaw. Pearson was tied and placed on a horse, while King and Wyatt headed back with him to the border, careful to avoid Mexican authorities.

King stood on the Mexican side of the border where he untied Pearson's feet. Then he pushed the criminal across the borderline where Wyatt, armed and with a warrant in his pocket, stood. Pearson was officially served and apprehended in the United States. An automobile was secured and Pearson was soon on his way to Los Angeles to stand trial.[33]

Another armed confrontation involving the famed lawman occurred in October of 1910, when 62-year-old Wyatt led a posse of 33 men into the Mojave Desert to take control of a potash field near Searles Lake. LAPD commissioner, Tom Lewis, had asked George Parsons, an old friend of Wyatt from the Tombstone days, to lead the posse. Parsons had a severe ankle injury, however, and Wyatt was selected to lead the charge.

The California Trona Company and Henry E. Lee & Associates both claimed legal ownership of the potash, which was used in explosives.

Earp, along with Lee and Lou Rasor, served as leaders of the posse organized to defend the claim of Henry Lee and Associates.

Anticipating a possible gun battle with the Trona

backers, Wyatt ordered his men to lie in the sagebrush throughout the night and be ready to open fire in case the opposing forces try to take control of the mining site.

Lou Rasor's court testimony, which didn't materialize until 1916, claimed that the morning after Wyatt and his men spent a nervous night in the brush keeping a watch out for trouble, Federal receiver, S.W. Austin and three armed men stormed into camp and ordered the Lee and Associates party to leave. Rasor said:

> "That Wyatt Earp, leader of the Lee armed forces snatched a rifle from one of the Austin men and then faced Austin's revolver, which he drew as the struggle started. Then Earp retreated to a hut and came back with rifle ready for action."

The legendary gunman's tough reputation proved to be no myth when Rasor boldly stated in court, "It was the most nervy thing, Earp's act, that I ever saw."

Fortunately, there was no blood shed. Austin and his men made no further resistance and joined the Lee party for breakfast. The two mining groups eventually went to trial in 1916 and took nearly three months of court time. The Trona Company walked away as victors.[34]

Wyatt was involved in a problematic incident in July of 1911, when he, Walter Scott, and Edward Dean were arraigned in Los Angeles for operating a bunco game. Wyatt pleaded innocence, that he had no idea that a rigged game was in the works. At a justice court hearing, charges against Wyatt were dropped.[35]

Perhaps in his final act as a peace officer with the Los Angeles Police Department, but one that is not well documented, Wyatt Earp allegedly worked for the LAPD's "pickpocket squad" during the early years of the popular National Orange Show (an annual event since 1911) in San Bernardino. James K. Guthrie, one of the city's prime civic leaders of the 20th century, met his western hero as a small boy in the early 1920s and said that Wyatt's job was to patrol the crowd so that nobody got out of hand.

A youngster at the time, Guthrie described Wyatt as "A robust man with a bristly white mustache. Earp lived up to my childhood fantasies". But what really thrilled the lad was that the famous Wyatt Earp took time out to share a story that he never forgot.

"I wasn't the fastest gun in the west. (Wild) Bill Hickock was." On the night that Hickock was shot in the back of the head while playing cards in Deadwood City, South Dakota on August 2, 1876, "in the split of a second before the bullet hit him, he managed to pull both of his guns and cock one of them."

Wyatt may have stretched the tale for Guthrie's benefit. Nevertheless, it was a cherished memory that the young boy never forgot.[36]

SAN BERNARDINO COUNTY DEPUTY SHERIFF

While Wyatt and Sadie were roosting at their desert

The Earp's cottage in Vidal, CA, where they spent happy winters for almost a quarter of a century. Sadie called it their "dream come true." From the Boyer Collection.

home in Vidal during the early 1920's, the Old West legend was presented with a San Bernardino County Deputy Sheriff's badge.

San Bernardino Sun columnist, L. Burr Belden, spoke with eye witnesses and wrote about this little known incident on June 25, 1961. Belden mentioned that the Earp's desert home initially was at Calzona, and only in the winter months. During the hot summer, when the temperatures built up to the point where it was uncomfortable to mine the Earps moved into Los Angeles.

Calzona was situated along a bumpy dirt road leading to the Colorado River ferry near Parker, Arizona. The small town consisted of a store, a railroad station, a post office and a small cluster of houses.

After a few years, the Earps moved four miles west

to Vidal where he figured in the capture of a "bad-man." The guy had gotten off the Los Angeles to Phoenix train and tried to clean Charles Bunnell's general store. Bunnell managed to escape and called Constable James Wilson to arrest the intruder, who was waving a gun.

Vidal was too far from the Sheriff's Office in San Bernardino in order to get help there, so Wilson asked Wyatt to back him up. The constable mapped out his plan for capture by asking Earp to go in the store's front door while he, Wilson, waited by the back door to arrest the scoundrel as he fled.

Wyatt had other plans though. He abruptly walked in the front door and ordered the intruder to hand over his gun. The command was obeyed. Earp grabbed the man's collar, pushed him out the door and called for Wilson.

Belden mentioned in his newspaper article: "The incident brought a lot of good-natured joshing with Constable Wilson on the receiving end—particularly when it was known that Earp was not armed".

Sheriff Walter Shay sent congratulations and commissioned Earp as a non-salaried deputy.[37]

Looking into primary sources such as oral interviews from eye witnesses can produce valuable historical information. But as Earp historian, Jim Petersen, pointed out, inaccuracies can also occur. Petersen, who has done a considerable amount of research on Wyatt's later years, looked into this "would be" robbery at Vidal. His findings came up with a letterhead

Wyatt Earp late in life.

indicating that the store owner was Charles Brownell (not Bunnell). Apparently, newspaperman/author Burr Belden, misheard the correct pronunciation from his informants. [38]

As for how Wyatt was deputized, this explanation gets a little fuzzy.

According to Belden, Wyatt was asked by Shay to stop in at his office near the old county jail on Court Street in San Bernardino the next time it was convenient so that he could be presented with the emblem. According to this account, the Earps stopped in town some weeks later on a day when Shay happened to be out of his office for other business. In Shay's absence, under sheriff Tom Carter presented the badge.

But Jack H. Brown, CEO of Stater Brothers Markets, clearly recalled his father, Deputy Sheriff, Jack H. Brown Sr., mentioning that he was involved with presenting Wyatt with the badge. Brown recalled:

> "My dad left the office he was station at in Victorville and went out where Wyatt was and gave him a badge. Back then, nobody ever rode out in the desert alone, so he most likely went out to meet Wyatt with either Shay or the under sheriff."[39]

Sun columnist, L. Burr Belden reported:

> "Last summer (1960) five one-time Calzona residents gathered for a reunion at the mobile-home of Lester Munn in Muscoy (a small unincorporated community near San Bernardino). Munn and his brother-in-law, Bradley, had the Earp mine under lease one year and took out a fair quantity of gold. All five of the former Calzonians recalled much about the tall, aging mine-operator who had been one of the nation's greatest breed of western law officers.

Although his health no longer permitted mining, Earp and his wife continued to spend the winter season in the area. It was by unanimous petition of the residents that the United States Postal Department and the Santa Fe Railroad changed the name from Drenan to Earp a year or so after the old marshal died. Things

Josephine (Sadie) Earp on the right in 1937. She's standing with Vinolia Earp Ackerman, sister of Mabel Earp Cason, who was Sadie's co-biographer with her sister. They stopped at Earp, CA, enroute to Tombstone to do research for Jose's memoir. From the Boyer Collection.

just didn't seem the same at the Bunnell store, where Wyatt's chair at the card table was no longer occupied by the tall, gray man with the slow, deliberate speech; the man respected so highly by his neighbors."[40]

THE REAL WYATT EARP

As the years were catching up with him, Wyatt rarely ventured away from home and visited only his closest friends. One such comrade was Charles Courtney "Charley" Welsh.

During an interview in 1989, Grace (Welsh) Spolidoro (1901-1999), Charlie's daughter, recalled her memories of Wyatt. "Oh, he was no saint!"But he was a good man and a good friend of the family." Affectionately nicknamed "Little Sister" by Wyatt, Spolidoro even spent a vacation with the Earps in San Diego one year and stayed at the Hotel del Coronado.

A 1995 photo of Grace Spolidoro at age 94.

Spolidoro, who was 88 years old at the time of the interview, had been well acquainted with both Wyatt and Sadie while she and her family lived in Needles. Wyatt frequently visited with the Welshes and was treated as a member of the family.

She recalled hearing many stories regarding Wyatt's past as frontier marshal, gambler, saloon keeper etc., but admitted that nobody in her family was really in awe of him because of those stories. Spolidoro insisted that Wyatt detested all the lies that had been written by dime novelists who portrayed him as a folk hero, as well as those who made him out to be nothing more than an outlaw.

There was no doubt in Spolidoro's mind as to how

the highly exaggerated legend of Wyatt Earp came about. "It was Sadie," she emphatically stated in reference to Wyatt's third wife, "who always interfered whenever Wyatt would talk with Stuart Lake. She was always interfering. She wanted him (Wyatt) to look like a churchgoing saint and blow things up. Wyatt didn't want that at all!"[41]

Ironically, when Lake's biography came out shortly after Wyatt's death, Sadie tried to sue the author. She had previously asked State Supreme Court Judge Jesse Curtis Sr. of San Bernardino for advice in an effort to prevent its publication. "All I could do," Curtis exclaimed years later, "is refer her to a lawyer—he was W.J. Hunsaker in Los Angeles—but apparently he couldn't do much, because the book came out soon after that."[42]

Remembered as tall, erect, with steely blue eyes that "could stare right through you", Wyatt was admired by the Welsh family as a gentleman who never acted disrespectful. However, he was also revered as a man who would not tolerate anyone showing disrespect, especially in front of women.

Spolidoro recalled one evening when several family members and friends were socializing at the Welsh home, and a man who obviously had too much to drink, was speaking obnoxiously to her niece. It didn't take long for Wyatt to put an end to the loudmouth's shenanigans. Without showing a hint of his intention, he suddenly stood up from his chair and with those piercing eyes and that low, deep voice that seemed to break off his words, said to the man, "You don't talk to a lady like that!" Everyone in the room was so stunned at Wyatt's reaction that no one made a sound.

During the handsome Wyatt's frequent visits to the Welsh home, he would always arrive neatly dressed

L. to R. Grace, parents Charlie and Elena Welsh. The other children are unidentified. Wyatt's friend, Grace (Welsh) Spolidoro in 1904. Caltado Collection.

and groomed, even after departing from his mining claims. His conversations with the women were cordial but rarely amounted to much more than small talk. On the other hand, Wyatt would spend hours talking with Charlie and the guys.

Spolidoro recalled her brother mentioning that ever since Wyatt's brothers were ambushed shortly after the gunfight with the Clantons and McLaurys in Tombstone, Wyatt would never sit inside a room with his back to a doorway or window. Charlie Welsh, perhaps influenced by his friend's cautious behavior, picked up the same habit and continued to do so throughout his life.

Such close friends were these two men, that when Wyatt and Sadie joined the rush to the Klondike gold fields during the late 1890s, Charlie soon followed with a herd of cattle. While there, Charlie worked as a cattle rancher while Wyatt ran the Dexter Saloon in Nome, Alaska.

As Wyatt entered his later years, he and Sadie began hitting on hard times. Having retained little of his profits from gambling halls that he once owned or from his various prospecting claims, they were barely getting by from relatively unsuccessful oil investments.

As for the Earp's money problems, Spolidoro refuses to place full blame on Wyatt's gambling. She insists that the primary cause of the Earp's troubles was Sadie's compulsive gambling! Supposedly, Sadie was so busy gambling with her friend, Mrs. Rose that she barely found the time to cook for Wyatt except for occasional meals of hot dogs and beans.[43]

In his highly acclaimed biography entitled, *Wyatt Earp: The Life Behind the Legend* (1997), author Casey Tefertiller gives further insight into Sadie's erratic behavior from an interview with Spolidoro's niece, Christenne Welsh. Pat Welsh, Christenne's uncle, told her of seeing Sadie enter the private card room in the back of a San Bernardino hotel where an illegal game took place.

"Uncle Pat said when he was selling the linen to the hotel, they'd see her coming and say, 'Well, we'll be able to more than eat today.' They'd take the money away from her. She didn't know how to play poker. People say Wyatt was the compulsive gambler—he was a normal gambler, I imagine. She was the compulsive one."[44]

"Oh, Say-dee!", Wyatt would say in that low voice of his whenever she embarrassed him with her sometimes outrageous comments to people, Mrs. Spolidoro recalled in reference to Sadie's sometimes eccentric behavior. "He really put up a lot with her."

The late John Earp, a distant relative of the Earp family who helped supply genealogical material for this book. Photo taken around 1994. He received a letter from a young boy in England during the late 1950s when the television show "Life and Times of Wyatt Earp" was popular. The letter was addressed to "Wyatt Earp, U. S. A."

When Charlie Welsh moved his family to Los Angeles a few years before he died in 1926, Wyatt and Sadie stayed with them until they found a small one-room motor court nearby to rent. However, Sadie, who was accused by author Stuart Lake as being mentally unstable, was finding it increasingly difficult to take care of Wyatt, who was now suffering from cancer. Fortunately, spending his last days in the warm confines of the Welsh home, Wyatt's needs were taken care of by Charlie's widow, Elena.

When Wyatt died on January 13, 1929—two

San Bernardino Historian Nick Cataldo and son Jay, at Earp, CA,

This may have been one of the Earps' cottages in Vidal, CA, where Wyatt and Sadie spent happy winters for almost a quarter of a century.

WYATT S. & JOSEPHINE EARP
MINING CLAIMS & DEEDS

IN SAN BERNARDINO COUNTY

This list of mining claims and deeds was transcribed from the original Index to Mines and Index to Deeds maintained in the San Bernardino County Archives, 777 E. Rialto Ave., San Bernardino, CA.

References to mining claims include the original location and description of claims made by the Earps on public lands. Also included in these references are "Proof of Labor" filings. These records show that a claim is being worked, and has not been abandoned. They indicate an investment of time and financial resources in the continued mining of the named claim.

References to the deed books are for those documents reflecting the sale or purchase of partial interest in specifically named mining claims.

Date Recorded	Name of Location	Name of Mine	Mining Book #	Page #
4-6-1905	W.S. & J.M. Earp	Lucky Day	43	13
4-6-1905	W.S. & J.M. Earp	Happy Day	43	13
6-28-1905	W.S. Earp	Cave	44	193
6-28-1905	W.S. Earp	Giant	44	194
11-13-1905	W.S. Earp	Copper Accident	43	375
11-13-1905	W.S. Earp	Hercules	43	376
11-13-1905	W.S. Earp	Colorado	43	376
12-20-1906	Josephine Earp	Jackuline	51	97
12-20-1906	Josephine Earp	Emil Jr.	51	97
12-20-1906	Josephine Earp	Turquoise	51	98
12-20-1906	Wyatt S. Earp, et al.	Mocking Bird	51	100
12-20-1906	Wyatt S. Earp, et al.	America	51	101
12-20-1906	Wyatt S. Earp, et al.	Last Chance	51	101
12-20-1906	Wyatt S. Earp, et al.	Thanksgiving	51	102
12-20-1906	Wyatt S. Earp, et al.	Virgil E.	51	102
12-20-1906	Wyatt S. Earp, et al.	Walter S.	51	103
12-20-1906	Wyatt S. Earp, et al.	Golden Gate	51	103
12-20-1906	Wyatt S. Earp, et al.	Marion	51	104
12-20-1906	Wyatt S. Earp, et al.	Henrietta	45	206
12-20-1906	Wyatt S. Earp, et al.	Sophie M.	45	206
12-20-1906	Wyatt S. Earp, et al.	Surprise	45	207
12-20-1906	Wyatt S. Earp, et al.	Rainbow	45	207
12-20-1906	Wyatt S. Earp, et al.	Edna L.	45	208
12-31-1906	Josephine S. Earp, et al.	Alice Mascot	53	35
1-2-1907	Wyatt Earp	Nutting	45	209
1-7-1907	Wyatt Earp, et al.	Silver Moon	51	294
1-7-1907	Wyatt Earp, et al.	Sunshine	51	294
1-7-1907	Wyatt Earp, et al.	Virginia	51	295
1-7-1907	Wyatt Earp, et al.	Golden Message	51	295
1-7-1907	Wyatt Earp, et al.	Evening Star	51	296

EARP MINING CLAIMS   **PAGE 2**

1-9-1908	Josephine Earp	Rosebud	64	31
1-9-1908	Josephine Earp	Grandma M.	64	32
1-9-1908	Josephine Earp, et al.	Louie L.	64	34
1-9-1908	Josephine Earp, et al.	Alice L.	64	35
2-5-1908	W.S. Earp, et al.	Humming Bird	64	238
2-5-1908	W.S. Earp, et al.	New Year	64	239
2-5-1908	W.S. Earp, et al.	Hattie L.	64	239
2-5-1908	W.S. Earp, et al.	Goodenough	64	240
2-5-1908	W.S. Earp, et al.	Alice L.	64	240
2-5-1908	W.S. Earp, et al.	Robert Ingersol	64	241
2-5-1908	W.S. Earp, et al.	My Joe	64	241
2-5-1908	W.S. Earp , et al.	Little Emil	64	242
2-5-1908	W.S. Earp, et al.	Venus	64	242
2-5-1908	W.S. Earp, et al.	Wisteria	64	243
2-5-1908	W.S. Earp, et al.	Gold Nugget	64	243
2-5-1908	W.S. Earp, et al.	Ida A.	64	244
2-5-1908	W.S. Earp, et al.	California	64	244
3-2-1908	Wyatt Earp, et al.	Nutting	65	225
1-8-1909	Wyatt Earp, et al.	Esperance	67	77
1-8-1909	Wyatt S. Earp	Cardwell	67	77
1-8-1909	Wyatt S. Earp	Ryland	67	78
1-8-1909	Wyatt S. Earp	Don Gara	67	78
1-8-1909	Wyatt S. Earp	Jess Martin	67	79
1-18-1909	Wyatt Earp, et al.	Happy Day, et al. (consolidation)	71	67-68
1-19-1909	Wyatt Earp, et al.	Happy Day group	74	52
1-19-1909	Josephine S. Earp	Diamond	76	408
1-19-1909	Josephine S. Earp	Emerald	76	408
1-19-1909	Josephine S. Earp	Garnet	76	409
1-19-1909	Josephine S. Earp	Pearl	76	409
1-20-1909	Josephine S. Earp	Marjorie Joel	76	436
1-22-1909	Josephine S. Earp	Mazuma	76	456
1-22-1909	Josephine S. Earp	Hopeful	76	457
1-22-1909	Josephine S. Earp	Friendship	76	457
1-22-1909	Josephine S. Earp	Abraham Lincoln	76	458
1-22-1909	Josephine S. Earp	May Flower	76	458
1-22-1909	Josephine S. Earp	George Washington	76	459
1-22-1909	Josephine S. Earp	Lilly	76	459
1-22-1909	Josephine S. Earp	Alice Beatrice	76	460
1-22-1909	Josephine S. Earp	Ruby	76	460
1-22-1909	Josephine S. Earp	Oakland Boy	67	152
1-1-1912	W. S. Earp	St. Francis	89	243
2-2-1912	W.S. Earp	Happy Day	93	57 & 58
2-24-1912	W.S. Earp, et al.	Nutting	93	133 & 134
12-31-1913	W.S. Earp, et al.	Dick Naylor, et al.	106	109 - 111
1-2-1914	J. Earp	Hattie	106	128
10-14-1914	W.S. Earp	Happy Day group	98	319
5-1-1917	Wyatt Earp, et al.	Europe	126	140

EARP MINING CLAIMS   **PAGE 3**

5-1-1917	Wyatt Earp, et al.	Irope	126	140
5-1-1917	Wyatt Earp, et al.	Earp	126	140
5-1-1917	Josephine Earp	Rainbow	126	140
12-26-1917	Josephine & Wyatt Earp	Happy Boy	Filed	
12-31-1919	W.S. Earp	Happy Day, et al.	144	392 & 393
1-29-1921	W. Earp	Horseshoe	151	145 & 146
7-5-1921	Wyatt Earp	Sister, et al.	152	19-23
3-13-1922	Wyatt Earp	Senator, 1-5	158*	115
3-13-1922	Wyatt Earp	Senator, 1-5	143	372-374

WYATT & JOSEPHINE EARP--Interest in mining claims (DEEDS)

Date Recorded	Grantor	Grantee	Deed Book #	Page #
6-21-1905	W.S. Earp	W.S. Abrams	320	76
9-25-1905	W.S. Earp	Emil Lehnhardt	390	10
9-28-1910	W. S. & I Abrams	W.S.Earp	466*	307
12-30-1912	John Quinn	W.S. Earp	521*	93
9-29-1915	Hattie Lehnhardt	Josephine Earp	578*	106
4-25-1918	W.S. Earp	J.M. Earp	423	210

*Books not available at the County Archives Center. Contact the San Bernardino County Recorder for assistance.

A total of 70 pages, including both mining claims and deeds, are available from the County Archives. There are 3 deeds and 1 mining claim, as indicated on the above list, that are not part of the Archives' collections and must be ordered from the San Bernardino County Recorder. The County Recorder may be contacted at the following address:

> San Bernardino County Recorder
> 222 W. Hospitality Lane
> San Bernardino, CA 92415-0022
>
> ATTN: Property Records Section

months shy of his eighty first birthday—the emotionally grieved Sadie left the funeral arrangements in the capable hands of Charlie's daughter-in-law, Alma. Two years later, Stuart N. Lake completed *Wyatt Earp: Frontier Marshal*, the book that created the Wyatt Earp legend.[45]

The following announcement appeared in the Needles Nugget on January 18, 1929:

EARP OF OLD FRONTIER DIES:

LIVED NEEDLES

"Mrs. Louis Welsh of Needles, who is staying in Los Angeles, attended the funeral of Wyatt Earp and will remain with Mrs. Earp, who is a very close friend, for a few days. Mrs. Welsh had planned to accompany the Earps to New York City next fall, when arrangements were to be concluded for publication of a history of Wyatt Earp's life by one of the big publishing houses. They were to have been guests of the late 'Tex' Rickard while in New York.

Wyatt Earp was well known in Needles years ago and made a number of trips out here since moving to Los Angeles. He came to Vidal occasionally for his health and to get away from the roaring city.

Los Angeles Examiner:

Wyatt Earp, last of the Herculean handful that pumped .45 caliber doses of militant peace into the young and lusty west, died Sunday morning at his home, 4004 West 17th Street.

He was 80 and when death knocked, it found the old lion of Tombstone, as ever, ready. They were what might be called old acquaintances, having played hide and seek with one another all over the west for nearly sixty years.

Mr. Earp had been confined to his bed for three months since his return from the Colorado river country, where he owned a copper mine.

Mr. Earp had been unconscious for several hours when he died. Another old-timer, Mr. Fred Shurtleff, who with a practice in the fashionable Wilshire and Beverly Hills neighborhoods, still carries his medicines in leather saddle bags, had been with him every moment for the last twelve hours.

A widow, Mrs. Sadie Earp, and a sister, Mrs. W. Edwards of Highland, survive.

Virgil, the eldest of the Earp brothers, died several years ago in Goldfield as an indirect result of wounds he received in that historic Tombstone "street fight" with the Clantons and the McLowries, Morgan, a younger brother, was murdered a few months after the battle. James died in Los Angeles about five years ago. Another brother, Warren, is long since dead. Newton, a half brother, died a few weeks ago. Mr. Earp was the last of the Earps and the last of the western frontier."[46]

Wyatt Earp, 1928, his last good portrait. Glenn Boyer Collection.

END NOTES

1. U. S. Pension Records, Declaration For Pension of James C. Earp, May 1, 1920.

2. San Bernardino Society of California Pioneers, *Minute Book A*, April 28, 1888, p. 45.

3. Rousseau, Sarah Jane, Rousseau Diary, 1864.

4. San Bernardino Public Library, Holman Curtis recollections, undated. Holman Curtis was only two years old at the time. Therefore, his recollections (in library's "Earp file" must have come from the older members of the wagon train.

5. Flood, John Henry, Flood Manuscript, an unpublished biography of Wyatt Earp, edited by Earl Chafin Press, 1926.

6. Boyer, Glenn G., Wyatt Earp: Legendary American, *True West Magazine*, 1993.

7. Lake, Stuart N., *Wyatt Earp: Frontier Marshal*, pp. 21-22, 1931.

8. IBID, pp. 23 and 24 and Casebier, Dennis G., *The Battle of Camp Cady*, p.1, 1972.

Author's note: There was an old railroad siding and community by the name of "Cadiz" in the Mojave Desert. It wasn't established until 1883 (the battle was in 1866).

9. Flood, John Henry, Flood Manuscript, an unpublished biography of Wyatt Earp, edited by Earl Chafin Press, 1926.

10. Boyer, Glenn G., Wyatt Earp: Legendary American, *True West Magazine*, 1993.

11. Lee A. Silva, Wyatt Earp—A biography of the Legend: *Vol. 1, The Cowtown Years*, p. 61, 2002

12. Edwards, Adelia, Memoirs, p. 1, written in 1932-1934, copyright, David H. Cruickshanks, Colton City Library, 1978.

13. Boyer, Glenn G., "Wyatt Earp: Legendary American", *True West Magazine*, 1993.

14. San Bernardino County Supervisor Minutes, Book D, p. 432.

15. Traywick, Ben T., *The Chronicles of Tombstone*, 1986.

16. Boyer, Glenn G., Wyatt Earp: Legendary American, *True West Magazine*, 1993.

17. San Bernardino City Directory, 1987.

18. Stephenson, Ed, "The Horton Grand; Time Warp in the Gas Lamp", *San Diego Magazine*, October, 1986. pp. 114-116.

19. Cilch, Kenneth R., Sr., *Wyatt Earp; The Missing Years*, pp. 30 and 31, 1998.

20. Boyer, Glenn G., *I Married Wyatt Earp*, pp. 132 and 133, 1976.

21. Stephenson, Ed, "The Horton Grand; Time Warp in the Gas Lamp", *San Diego Magazine*, October, 1986. pp.114-121, pp. 229-233. Oral Interview with Bob Earp, December, 1986.

22. Boyer, Glenn G., *I Married Wyatt Earp*, pp. 140--142 , 1976. Also, Chafin, Earl, "Wyatt's Woman (She Married Wyatt Earp), edited 1998.

23. San Francisco News letter and *California Advertiser* (newspaper), April 2, 1892.

24. Daggett, Nathalie, Oral Interview with Marsha Patrick, 1993.

25. Clyde, Robert, Oral interview with author, 1990.

26. Edwards, Adelia, Memoirs, p. 6, written in 1932-1934, copyright, David H. Cruickshanks, Colton City Library, 1978.

27. Tefertiller, Casey, *Wyatt Earp: The Life Behind the Legend*, p. 309, 1997.

28. Chaput, Don, *Virgil Earp: Western Peace Officer*, p. 213, 1994.

29. Holladay, Fred, "As Rich as Vanderbilt", *Heritage*

Tales, 1979.

30. Belden, L. Burr, "History in The Making", *San Bernardino Sun-Telegram*, April 23, 1956.

31. San Bernardino County Archives, Index to mines and Deeds for Wyatt and Josephine Earp,

32. Hickey, Michael M., *The Death of Warren Baxter Earp: A Closer Look*, pp. 400-401, 2000.

33. King, A.M. as told to Lea F. McCarty, "Wyatt Earp's Million Dollar Shotgun Ride," *True West*, August 1958, p.p16-17. Tefertiller, Casey, *Wyatt Earp: The Life Behind the Legend*, p.312, 1997.

34. San Bernardino County Courts, Waymire and Trona trial manuscripts.

35. Boyer, Glenn G., *I Married Wyatt Earp*, p. 236, 1976.

36. Mauel, Ed., "Orange Show Blossoms in Book", *San Bernardino Sun*, July 31, 1994.

37. Belden, L. Burr, "Wyatt Earp's Desert Home Saved For Public", *San Bernardino Sun - Telegram* (newspaper), June 25, 1961. A short time after Wyatt died in 1929, the small desert town of Drenan, located within a few miles of Vidal, was renamed "Earp".

38. Petersen, Jim, Oral interview, June 11, 2006. Petersen's research came up with a letterhead from Vidal stating, "December 12, 1914…Vidal Mercantile Company…Dealers in General Merchandise…"Brownell and Son". Brownell ran the store into the 1930s.

39. Brown, Jack H., Oral interview with author, April, 2006. Deputy Sheriff Jack H. Brown, Sr., worked for the San Bernardino County Sheriff's Department from 1919 until 1946. This testimony of how the badge was presented obviously differs from what L. Burr Belden's informants told him.

40. Belden, L. Burr, "Wyatt Earp's Desert Home Saved for Public", *San Bernardino Sun - Telegram* (newspaper), June 25, 1961. A short time after Wyatt died in 1929,

the small desert town of Drenan, located within a few miles of Vidal, was renamed "Earp".

41. Spolidoro, Grace, Oral Interview with author, 1989.

42. Saulsbury, James M., "Famed Earp Family Well-Known in San Bernardino County Area, *San Bernardino Sun-Telegram* (newspaper), April 17, 1957.

43. Spolidoro, Grace, Oral Interview with author, 1989.

44. Tefertiller, Casey, *Wyatt Earp: The Life Behind the Legend*, p.320--322, 1997.

45. Spolidoro, Grace, Oral Interview with author, 1989.

46. "Earp of Old Frontier Dies" *Needles Nugget* (newspaper), January 18, 1929.

Chapter Five

A LIFE CUT SHORT
MORGAN SETH EARP

Morgan Seth Earp was one of the key figures in the well known "Gunfight at the O.K. Corral". And whenever the Earp brothers are mentioned in books or in movies, his name comes up. Unfortunately, because he died at such a young age — not quite 31, there isn't a whole lot of biographical information about the man.

What we do know is

This is the only known authentic photo of Morgan Earp and was provided by the grand-niece and nephew of Morgan's common-law-wife, Louisa Houston Earp. From the Boyer Collection.

that Morgan Earp was born in Pella, Iowa, on April 24, 1851 and as a 13 year old, traveled with his family from Iowa to San Bernardino, California in 1864.[1]

When the oldest boys—Newton, James and Virgil—were off fighting for the union Army during the Civil War, young Wyatt and Morgan were left to tend the family farm. The two brothers would grow up close with a shared desire for adventure and a disdain for farming.

All of the Earp brothers were good fighters and had few problems holding their ground in facing trouble. However, sister Adelia gave a little glimpse on sometimes over sensitive personality of Morgan.

> "Morgan was in a fight with a buffalo hunter one day and it would have come to shooting if Newton had not gotten between them and talked them into shaking hands. Morgan had a terrible temper while Newton was always very even in his ways."[2]

Morgan accompanied the rest of the Earps back to the Midwest in 1868. A few years later, he followed his older brothers on various adventures on the western frontier until they all met in Tombstone in December, 1879.[3]

Morgan went back to California sometime in 1880 as the census for San Bernardino County on July 23rd of that year indicated that Morgan and Louisa were staying with Morg's parents in Temescal.[4]

The following excerpts from letters written by Morgan's wife, Louisa Houston to her sisters, Kate and Agnes, shed some light on the period when the California bound Earps lived in Temescal and about Morgan. The original documents are in the Glenn G. Boyer collection. Copies were made via correspondence with the late San Bernardino and Earp historian, Fred Holladay.

"Temescal, San Bernardino California

May the 11th 1880

Dear Sister Kate,

Your letter of the 29th is at hand with much welcome for I am in deed very glad to hear from you and I thank you much for your picture. It is very good picture but I don't think it looks a bit natural but I knew it was you the moment I put my eyes upon it. My husband thinks you are a great deal better looking than me but I can't see the point for I think I look very well to have weathered the storm I have during the past seven years. My face has held its own pritty well, you can bet for I have suffered death a thousand times and have often longed for it. Although I can never get well again, I have much hopes of getting strong and able to get around like other folks, that is if I live long enough and I begain to think I am going to live as long as any boddy for I guess I am pretty tough after all. Although it is very painfull for me to be on my feet much, I manage to get around and do considerable work. Me and my old man is all alone today for the old folks have gone to town thirty miles away to be gone a week so we are going to have a good time. There is a dance tomorrow night and we are going. I never made much of a success at dancing but I shall go. I have been here over two months and have only been off the place once.

.... Give my love to all from your Sister Louisa Houston to Kate Houston[5]

"Temescal San Bernardino Co.

California

July the 19th 1880

Dear Sister Agnes:

Your kind and most welcome letter is at hand. I am very glad to hear from you and to hear you are all well. This has me quite well at present and I sincerely hope when this comes to hand it will find you all enjoying the best of health. .... My husband starts for Arizona in the morning. I am going to stay here for the present with his parents. They do not want me to go and I do not want to go so I think I will stay here this summer. ...

From your sister Louisa Houston to Agnes Houston[6]

Temescal Mountains California

August the 30th 1880

Dear Sister Agnes:

Your kind and most welcome letter is at hand. I am very glad to hear from you and to hear that you are all well and that mothers health is improving. My health is about the same, not very much improved. I thought at first I was improving fast but I think I am about on a standstill for I do not see much improvement as I have had the rumatisism a great deal lately but I do not mind that much as it has become a second nature to me to be sick.

... My husband is still in Arizona and he writes that it has rained steady there for sixty days during the day time, but at night it quits. ...I was up in San Bernardino when your letter came and that was two weeks as it came the day after I left and I stayed for two weeks. I went to get my teeth fixed but could not get them fixed there and so I shall have to go to Riverside about twenty miles off. I shall go tomorrow and I dread the ride very much but it is a beautiful little town. The main avenue, as it is called, is eight miles long. The road is double two roads running side by side with a row or ornamental trees running between the roads and also on each side with a row of ornamental trees running between the roads and also on each side and each side is laid out in squares owned by different people. Then there is evergreens and ornamental trees of every description, then their is fountains, and flower gardens and orchards until you will get tired of looking and a great many of these flowers grow into large trees and if their houses are only one story, they will hide them from view."[7]

When Morgan returned to Tombstone, he replaced Wyatt as a shotgun messenger for Wells Fargo when the former became deputy sheriff. And shortly before the shootout with the Clantons and McLaurys on Oc-

Louisa Houston Earp, date unknown. She was the common-law-wife of Morgan Earp at Tombstone and before. From the Boyer Collection.

tober 26, 1881, he was deputized by city marshal, Virgil Earp.[8]

Two months after the gunfight, Virgil was seriously wounded in an assassination attempt by the Clanton gang. Sensing further danger for the Earps, Morgan feared for the safety of his wife, Louisa, who had moved to Tombstone. So he sent her back to be with his parents, who had recently moved to Colton, California. However, Morgan himself chose to remain in Tombstone to support Virgil and Wyatt in the event that more trouble was on the way. And that's exactly what happened.

Around 10:00 P.M. on Saturday, March 18, 1882, Morgan was killed by gunfire while playing pool with Wyatt at Campbell and Hatch Billiard parlor on Tombstone's Allen Street.

Adelia Earp Edwards, commented on Morgan's final days and Louisa's reaction to her husband's murder.

"And we used to wonder about Morgan's wife too. When she heard he had been murdered, she went off to Arizona to bring his body back to Colton and only stayed with us for a few weeks more after he was put to rest. She was a real, sad lady. I recall best that sad look in her eyes. But she was a fine person and a stunning looker, and she was waiting for Morg to come back from Tombstone when she heard. She just fell down on the floor and sobbed and sobbed. She lived in Tombstone a short time, but Morg sent her home to wait until they were ready to come home. I guess he was worried for her there. She was a clever young lady, had been to good schools. She just went away. We just don't know what became of her.[9]

Morgan's body was taken by wagon the next day to the railhead in Benson. From there, his remains were accompanied by older brother, Jim, to his parents' home in Colton.

Morgan was initially buried in Colton's old cemetery, near Slover Mountain. When the Southern Pacific Railroad established its right of way through that site in 1892, his body was reburied in the city's new Hermosa Cemetery.[10]

Photo of headstone of Morgan S. Earp in the Hermosa Cemetery in Colton, CA. Photo by author.

END NOTES

1. Edwards, Jean Whitten, *Earp Family Genealogy*, Breckenridge, Texas: Beck Printing, 1991.

2. Edwards, Adelia, Memoirs, p. 4, written in 1932-1934, copyright, David H. Cruickshanks, 1978.

3. Traywick, Ben T., *The Chronicles of Tombstone*, 1986.

4. Census for San Bernardino County, July 23, 1880.

5. Houston, Louisa, letter written to her sister Kate. The original correspondence is in the Glenn G. Boyer collection and a copy was given to the late San Bernardino/Earp historian, Fred Holladay in 1984.

6. Houston, Louisa, letter written to her sister Agnes. The original correspondence is in the Glenn G. Boyer collection and a copy was given to the late San Bernardino/Earp historian, Fred Holladay in 1984.

7. IBID

8. Traywick, Ben T., *The Chronicles of Tombstone*, 1986.

9. Edwards, Adelia, Memoirs, p. 6, written in 1932--1934, copyright, David H. Cruickshanks, 1978.

10. Holladay, Fred, *The Earp Clan in San Bernardino County*, Heritage Tales, p.46, 1978.

Chapter Six

WARREN BAXTER EARP:
A TRAGIC LIFE

Almost 19 years after the famous street fight in Tombstone, often referred to as the "Gunfight at the O.K. Corral", Wyatt Earp's youngest brother, Warren, was gunned down in a Willcox, Arizona saloon. Some newspapers reported that the killing was the result of a feud that had existed since the Tombstone troubles between the Earps and the cowboys in the early 1880's. Others insisted that Warren, the eighth of ten children and the baby brother of the Earp clan, was a troublemaker and had provoked the fight.

Warren Baxter Earp was 9 years old when the family came to San Bernardino from Pella, Iowa, in 1864 on a wagon train led by his father, Nicholas Porter "Nick" Earp. The caravan included three other Pella families—the Rousseaus, Hamiltons and Curtises.[1]

A diary of the trip was recorded by Sarah Jane Rousseau and her entry on November 24, 1864 described a fight between Warren and a boy named Jimmy Hatten. This was not only his first documented altercation; it also turned out to be a prelude for the lifestyle that would plague Warren to his last days.[2]

The Earps arrived in San Bernardino on December 17, 1864 after seven months on the road. They remained in that vicinity—living on a small farm along the banks of the Santa Ana River in what is now Redlands—for about four years until 1868, when they headed back to the Midwest.[3]

Warren Earp at age 25. Courtesy of San Bernardino Historical and Pioneer Society.

During the 1870s, Warren's older brothers led adventuresome lives—traveling to places like Wichita, Dodge City and Montana. They engaged in such business adventures as buffalo hunting, stage driving and law enforcement. The elder Earp boys also met colorful personalities like Doc Holliday, Bat Masterson and Luke Short. Young Warren, on the other hand, had to stick close to home.

So when the Earp family made the difficult journey back to San Bernardino in 1877, Warren was with them. He was 22 years old and his older brothers were long out on their own. Knowing of the daring lives his brothers were leading, Warren must have longed to get out on his own and experience life's offerings. But this would not happen permanently for a while. In the Great Register for San Bernardino County for May 5, 1879, Warren was listed as a "farmer" while living with his parents in Temescal.[4]

In December of 1880, Nick Earp again moved, this time to the sleepy town of Colton. He resurrected an old saloon and renamed it the "Gem" and Warren worked there as a bartender.[5]

After the bloody shooting affair in Tombstone on October 26, 1881, and its aftermath—which included the murder of Morgan the following March—Warren was devastated. He had spent a few months visiting his brothers there just prior to the shootout and now he was back in Colton, feeling helpless. Against his grieving parents' wishes, he returned to Tombstone and joined a posse led by Wyatt and Doc Holliday, tracking down Morgan's killers. He later fled Arizona with Wyatt and Doc to escape prosecution for the assassins' deaths.

When Warren returned to the San Bernardino area a year later, he became prone to heavy drinking, fits of temper and repeated bouts of violence. Nonetheless, he was usually able to emerge from sticky situations with relative ease as the following newspaper accounts from 1883 and 1884 exemplify:

The Silver City Enterprise for June 8, 1883 reported: "Warren Earp, one of the most quarrelsome of the Earp brothers, recently got into a shooting scrape in Colton, San Bernardino County, California, and escaped officers, who were in hot pursuit of him at last accounts. Nine shots were exchanged between Earp and a Mexican named Belarde, neither was seriously injured. The Mexican was arrested."[6]

The Tucson *Arizona Daily Star* mentioned on April 11, 1884:

"According to the *San Bernardino Index*, Warren Earp has been getting into trouble again. It says: "Warren Earp of Colton, while intoxicated, entered the French restaurant on "D" Street (in San Bernardino) and called for a supper. While his order was being prepared and before it was served, he became very noisy and tried to break the bottles in the caster. The night steward gathered up a big, heavy water bottle to defend himself with, but unfortunately before he could use it, Earp struck him on the arm with a pickle bottle, shattering the bottle and lacerating the waiter's arm and hand in a fearful manner. Officer Thomas was called in, when he placed Earp under arrest, and this morning he was taken before recorder Morgan, who fined him $25."[7]

Warren left the San Bernardino area a short time

later according to Dan Tripp who was interviewed for an article in the San Jacinto Valley Register on May 1, 1953. Tripp recalled seeing Warren in the town of San Jacinto in 1886. He described the hotheaded Earp brother "as a big man, moustached and handsome, who spent his days (and nights) drinking and gambling". Tripp's brother, Will, carried the mail at the time and frequently stayed overnight in Colton where he got to know the family well. A few years later, Warren Earp was back in San Bernardino area and got himself involved in at least two saloon brawls.[8]

The San Bernardino Weekly Courier for December 3, 1892, mentioned that Warren took on two Latino men at the M. and O. Saloon on Third Street in San Bernardino, swinging a wooden stick at both and slightly cracking the head of the one named Juan Bustamente. All three were arrested, but Nick Earp, who was the much respected justice of the peace in Colton, bailed Warren out of jail the same night.

The next day the other two men were fined, while his son was released without paying a cent.[9]

The second bar fight had a similar outcome. The *San Bernardino Times-Index* mentioned on August 18, 1893, that Warren commenced harassing a man named Steele by calling him "a filthy name". Steele struck Warren, who became so enraged that he stabbed Steele a couple times in the back. In court, Judge Peck sentenced Steele to a $10 fine or ten days in jail. Warren was again dismissed with no fine or jail time.

After the latter incident, there were protests that Judge Peck had made a "grave mistake". Colton was

*Warren Earp in 1890. From the album of his sister, Adelia. The Boyer
Collection.*

pretty much fed up with Warren Earp. Even his father,
who clearly loved Warren, was losing faith in his son.
He sent him out on his own with the hope that Warren
would leave his trouble making cronies behind and
find salvation elsewhere.[10]

Warren moved on to Yuma, Arizona, where he
picked up a job driving stages. But only two months
later, he was in trouble again. The *Arizona Prospector*
reported on November 11, 1893:

> "Warren Earp, one of the notorious brothers
> who terrorized Tombstone several years ago,
> was arrested today for assaulting Prof. Behrens.
> Earp invited the professor to walk across the
> bridge with him and when half way across he
> seized Behrens by the throat and attempted to

throw him off the bridge. Behrens resisted successfully and finally induced Earp to let him alone by promising to give him $25."[11]

For the next seven years Warren was in and out of trouble, unable to hold a steady job. Then on July 7, 1900, his tragic life came to an end in Willcox, Arizona, when he was killed by a cowboy named Johnny Boyett.

Warren was unarmed other than a pocket knife when his body was examined. However, at the inquest Boyett was absolved of any crime.[12]

END NOTES

1. Rousseau, Sarah Jane, Rousseau Diary, 1864.

2. IBID

3. Lake, Stuart N., *Wyatt Earp: Frontier Marshal*, 1931.

4. Great Register for San Bernardino County, May 5, 1879.

5. Holladay, Fred, "The Earp Clan in San Bernardino County", *Heritage Tales*, p. 26, 1978.   H o l l a d a y quotes the May 15, 1887 issue of The *Colton Semi-Tropic*, newspaper.

6. Hickey, Michael M., *The Death of Warren Baxter Earp: A Closer Look, 2000.*

Hickey quotes on page xxvii from the *Silver City Enterprise* for June 8, 1883

7. IBID

Hickey quotes on page xxvii from the *Tucson Arizona Daily Star* for April 11, 1884.

8. *San Jacinto Valley Register*, (newspaper), May 1, 1953.

9. *San Bernardino Weekly Courier*, December 3, 1892.

10. *San Bernardino Times - Index*, (newspaper), August 18, 1893.

11. *Arizona Prospector*, (newspaper), November 11, 1893.

12. Holladay, Fred, "Warren Earp: The Tragic One", *Heritage Tales*, 1979.

Chapter Seven

THE FORGOTTEN EARP BOYS

JAMES COOKSEY EARP

So much has been written about Old West legend Wyatt Earp and his brothers, Virgil and Morgan. Their exploits have been written about and portrayed in movies seemingly a million times.

But how many people have even heard of older brother Jim? Virtually nothing is ever mentioned about him. The life of this somehow "forgotten" Earp began on June 28, 1841, in Hartford, Kentucky, when James Cooksey became the first born child of Nicholas Porter and Virginia Ann Cooksey Earp.

After the birth of Virgil two years lat-

James Earp, from a photo found in the album of Adelia Earp. From the Boyer Collection.

er, the family (which included Newton, a half brother born during Nick's first marriage) moved from Kentucky to Monmouth, Illinois. The Earps settled there just long enough to see the birth of Wyatt in 1848 and then moved across the Mississippi River to Pella, Iowa, where two sons and a daughter were born to them: Morgan, in 1851; Warren, in 1855; and Adelia, in 1861.[1]

On May 25, 1861, shortly after the Confederate attack on Fort Sumter, Jim enlisted with the Union army's Company F, Seventh Illinois Infantry. Before long, Newton and Virgil joined him.

While battling it out with the rebels at Fredericktown, Missouri, on October 8, 1862, Jim suffered a gunshot wound in his left shoulder. According to his pension records, the injury would be severe enough that he would never have full use of his left arm again. And immediately after the incident Jim was sent back to his home in Iowa on convalescent furlough. There he waited for his discharge, which came on March 22, 1863.[2]

Forever seeking adventure and looking to make a buck, Jim leaped at the chance to go out West when his folks decided to pull up stakes from their Iowa home for a move to Southern California a year later.

Always the opportunist, by the time the wagon train—which included Wyatt, Morgan, Warren, and 3-year-old Adelia—reached Nevada, Jim abandoned ship and headed for the boom town of Austin. Bum shoulder and all, it was probably here that he picked up gambling as a profession, a pretty formidable skill eventually passed on to his younger brothers.

In between occasional visits with his family, who had settled down on a farm just outside of San Bernardino in December of 1864, Jim moseyed on to Montana for a spell where he worked as a gambler while the rest of the Earp clan for various reasons, were making plans for a move back to the Midwest.[3]

While reuniting with his family, which had settled down in Lamar, Missouri, a rather mysterious side of Jim's life first came to light.

Photo of James Earp's grave in Mountain View Cemetery in San Bernardino. Author's Collection.

He married Nellie Bartlett Ketchum, who was either widowed or a divorcee, in Illinois on April 18, 1873. According to his pension records, they had two children: Frank, born in 1874 and Hattie, in 1875.[4]

Some confusion surfaced while author Frank Waters was recording the memoirs of Virgil's wife, Allie, for his book *The Earp Brothers of Tombstone*. Allie claimed that Jim had a step-daughter named Hattie about 16-years-old living in Tombstone in 1880, which the census for that year confirmed. The killing of Jim Earp's stepson, Frank Ketchum, by Apaches in 1885, was also listed in the *Tombstone Epitaph*. Frank was a freighter at the time and at least in his very late teens by then. Why information on Jim was so ambiguous one can't say as it didn't appear that there was reason to conceal anything.

Then, another bit of controversy arose while Jim, Wyatt, and their wives were living in Wichita, Kansas. Miller and Snell, authors of *Great Gunfighters of The Kansas Cow Towns, 1867-1886*, claimed that Jim's wife was involved in the "sporting" profession. The authors reported in their book that "Bessie Earp, wife of Jim, was fined in Wichita police court in May, 1874, for being a prostitute. So was Sally Earp, who apparently shared the same dwelling, but for whom no other identification has been found. Bessie and Sally were each fined $8 and $2 court costs. Sally's name appears regularly in the city's prostitute file list February 1875 and Bessie's through March 1875."

As it turned out, it was " Betsy" Earp who was mentioned in the official report. Miller and Snell stated that "Bessie" was the "Betsy" arrested for prostitution. While there is no proof regarding this assumption, its highly probable that "Bessie" was misheard by the census enumerator for Betsy. It is also a strong possibility that the Sally who was handcuffed may have been misheard for "Seally", which is what family members' associates called Wyatt's second wife, Celia Ann Blaylock.[5]

Meanwhile, after a series of misadventures, Nick Earp moved his family in Missouri westward once again in 1877. Virgil and his wife accompanied his parents as far as Prescott, Arizona, while the rest of the family continued on to Temescal, California. During that time Jim teamed up with young Wyatt while heading for the Kansas cow towns of Wichita and Dodge City. There the likable gambler tended bar while his younger brother developed a reputation as a tough lawman.[6]

In 1879 Virgil, newly appointed as Deputy U.S. Marshal for the Arizona Territory, wrote to Jim and Wyatt in Dodge, urging them to meet him at a new silver mining town called Tombstone, as there appeared to be unlimited opportunities. Before long, the boys were on their way from Kansas and Morgan left California to join them.

Soon after their arrival in town, the Earp boys filed several mining claims. Jim began working at Vogan's Bowling Alley and then found a job as a bartender at the newly opened Sampling Room. Wyatt immediately gained an interest in some gambling layouts while also working as shot gun messenger for Wells Fargo. Morgan eventually took over that job when Wyatt was appointed Pima County Deputy Sheriff.[7]

Two years after the brothers arrival in Tombstone, Wyatt, Virgil and Morgan had their celebrated "O.K. Corral" shootout with the Clantons and the McLaurys which would forever engrave their names in western history.

There is little doubt that Jim would have stood along side his brothers during the confrontation, had it not been for the near crippling gunshot wound (although he could sure deal those cards) suffered during the war twenty years earlier.

With their blond hair, cool blue eyes, and drooping mustaches, this close knit quartet, identical in appearance except for Jim, standing a bit shorter than his six-foot tall younger brothers, would have really been a sight to behold. It is due to this gunfight that the names of Wyatt, Virgil, and Morgan Earp have been immortalized in folklore and legend, while the name of James Earp has wallowed into oblivion.[8]

After the shooting fiasco, Morgan was murdered, Virgil encountered a nearly fatal ambush and there were retaliated killings of members of the cowboy gang.

Along with Wyatt, Jim high-tailed it out of Tombstone and explored Idaho's short lived "Coeur d'Alene Gold Rush" and operated the White Elephant Saloon at Eagle City.[9]

By 1885, Jim was back in California and apparently explored for a while the silver mining town of Calico. Located out in the Mojave Desert portion of San Bernardino County, silver had been discovered there four years earlier and the boom was just starting its downhill slide when he arrived. There was a big celebration at the Odd Fellows Ball in late April, 1885. Two of the attendees were Jim and his wife, Bessie.[10]

A short time later, they joined his folks who were

now making their home in Colton, California. During the next few years, while Virgil and Nick established themselves as constable and justice of the peace in Colton, Jim worked for a while as a stage driver around the area before opening up the Club Exchange Saloon on "D" Street in San Bernardino with a man named J. H. Anderson.[11]

Adelia Earp Edwards recorded in her memoirs:

> I heard many of the tales from Jim and Bessie in the 1880s after they had come back (to California) from Arizona. Bessie was not a happy woman then and it affected her health. She died in a few years, and I reckon her poor heart was broke, what with her daughter (Hattie) running off like that in Tombstone, and then she never knowing what became of her for a long time, and the boy died so young, too. But there were good times when we all got together and had a laugh about the funny things gone by."[12]

When Bessie died from a sudden illness on January 22, 1887, Jim hit the road again, taking his gambling and bartending talents to Montana and then San Francisco before finally settling down for good in San Bernardino in the early 1900s.[13]

While taking up quarters at various locations in town (409 D Street, 421 3rd Street, and 340 4th Street), Jim worked as a laborer until paralysis and high blood pressure forced him into retirement. Becoming more dependent on care from his sister, Adelia, he moved in with her family.[14]

As Jim's health worsened, the aging gambler needed a full time nurse, a role provided by his grandniece,
Hildreth Hallowell, who was living at 1236 West 53rd
Street, in Los Angeles. He died there on January 25,
1926, from a stroke at the age of 84.

When James Cooksey Earp's body was returned to
San Bernardino, Adelia, paid for the funeral expenses.
He was laid to rest in the "Bubah Plot" at Mountain
View Cemetery.[15]

NEWTON JASPER EARP

Newton Jasper Earp was born in Ohio County, Kentucky on October 7, 1837. He was the first born son of
Nicholas Earp, the only male by his first wife, Abigail
Storm, and the half-brother to the "fighting Earps".
Newton is rarely mentioned in books and is practically
nonexistent in the multitude of Earp movies made over
the years. There is not a whole lot of information on the
man and there is no evidence that he ever set foot in
Southern California. But Newton was part of the famous Earp Clan and is certainly worthy to be included
in this book.

Newton enlisted in Company F, 4th Cavalry, Iowa
Volunteers on November 11, 1861, and was mustered
out as Fourth Corporal on June 26, 1865, in Louisville,
Kentucky.[16] He married Nancy Jane Adam in Marion
County, Missouri, on September 12, 1865, and had five
children: Effie May, born on May 6, 1870; Wyatt Clyde,
born on August 25, 1872; Mary Elizabeth, born on August 25,1875; Alice Abigail, born on December 18, 1878;
and Virgil Edwin, born on April 19, 1880.[17]

Newton Earp, half-brother of the Fighting Earp brothers who were at Tombstone, shown with his wife Nancy Jane Adam Earp. From the Boyer Collection.

According to his pension records, Newton was described as 5 feet eight inches tall, blue eyes, brown hair, and auburn complexion.[18] His sister, Adelia, recalled in her memoirs that the oldest Earp brother was a farmer most of his life, was hard working, and a community leader. He and his wife, Nancy, were strict old-fashioned Methodists. In fact, they were a little too religious for the rest of the family.

"Sort of like religious fanatacs. We were all trying to be good Christians but we never did match up to Newton's family. This religious business caused some trouble with us and after Morgan was murdered we hardly ever did have much more to do with them, even after Newton moved to California. That was about 1900, I reckon. So I hardly got to know Newton at all."[19]

Newton was instrumental in founding the Garden City Methodist Church and was elected Garden City, Kansas' first marshal. After many years of farming, he moved his family to a ranch in Paradise Valley, Nevada. Nancy died there on March 29, 1898. After her death, Newton lived in the Napa County Veteran's Home for a short while and then sometime in 1900, moved to the Fruitridge area of Sacramento. In 1912, he applied for a Civil War pension and lived out the remainder of his life in Sacramento.[20]

Newton Earp died on December 18, 1928, at the age of 91 and is buried in Sacramento's East Lawn Cemetery.[21]

END NOTES

1. Holladay, Fred, "The Earp Clan in San Bernardino County", p.46, *Heritage Tales*, 1978.
2. Examining Surgeon's Certificate, October 21, 1874.
3. Boyer, Glenn G., *I Married Wyatt Earp*, p.57, 1976.
4. U.S. Pension records, Declaration for Pension of James C. Earp, May 1, 1920.
5. Miller, Nyle H. and Snell, Joseph W., *Great Gunfighters of The Kansas Cowtowns: 1867-1886*, 1963.
6. Boyer, Glenn G., *I Married Wyatt Earp*, p.57, 1976.
7. Traywick, Ben T., *The Chronicles of Tombstone*, p.28,1986.
8. Turner, Alford E., *The O.K. Corral Inquest*, 1981.
9. Boyer, Glenn G., *I Married Wyatt Earp*, p.125, 1976.
10. *Calico Print*, (newspaper) May 3, 1885.
11. San Bernardino County Directory, 1887.
12. Edwards, Adelia, Memoirs, p. 6, written in 1932-1934, copyright, David H. Cruickshanks, Colton City Library, 1978.
13. Great Voter Registration, 1908.
14. San Bernardino County Directories, 1914, 1920, and 1924.
15. Department of Health, Certificate Copy of Local Record of Death of James Cooksey Earp. April 6,1926.
16. Death certificate and pension records(1912) for Newton J. Earp.
17. Edwards, Jean Whitten, *Earp Family Genealogy*,Breckenridge, Texas: Beck Printing, 1991.
18. Death certificate and Pension records (1912) for Newton J. Earp.
19. Edwards, Adelia, Memoirs, p. 3 and 4, written in 1932-1934, copyright, David H. Cruickshanks, Colton City Library, 1978.
20. Traywick, Ben T., Oral interview, May 25, 2006.

21. Edwards, Jean Whitten, *Earp Family Genealogy*, Breckenridge, Texas: Beck Printing, 1991.

Chapter Eight

THE EARP WOMEN

VIRGINIA ANN COOKSEY
"MOTHER EARP"

Imagine being a pioneer mother to nine children while also being married to a man who is as restless and cantankerous as they come. That's the situation in which Virginia Ann Cooksey (1821-1893) found herself in the years after her 1840 wedding to Nicholas Porter (Nick) Earp.

Five of her children were the legendary "fighting Earp boys"—James, Virgil, Wyatt, Morgan, and Warren. There were three girls—Martha, Virginia, and Adelia—but only the last one lived to adulthood. She also raised a stepson, Newton.[1]

Virginia Ann lived a full life in a time which we can today only imagine. A life as wife, mother and pioneer woman, she was raised on

Virginia Ann Cooksey Earp. Mother of the Earp Clan. Courtesy San Bernardino Historical and Pioneer Society.

the frontier in Kentucky and lived out her final years in Southern California. "Mother Earp" was a loving role model for her children and a constant companion—in good times and bad—to her husband.

As matriarch of the Earp clan, Virginia Ann endured more than her share of excitement. She supported her adventuresome husband with two overland trips from the Midwest to the San Bernardino Valley, in 1864 and again during the late 1870s.[2]

During the first journey, her husband led a caravan of four families from Pella, Iowa to San Bernardino, California. One of the wagon train participants, Sarah Jane Rousseau, wrote a daily journal during the rugged seven month ordeal. Her comments portray Nick as profane and hardheaded. Nine-year-old Warren was reported fighting with other boys.[3]

Some years later, the notoriety of Virgil, Wyatt and Morgan—plus their unwillingness to back down from a fight—helped produce the infamous "Gunfight at the O.K. Corral" in Tombstone, Arizona on October 26, 1881. The aftermath of the fiasco included the murder of Morgan and a nearly fatal crippling injury for Virgil.[4]

Warren, the hot headed youngest son, got into one too many brawls and was gunned down in Wilcox, Arizona in 1900.[5]

Mother Earp was deeply loved by her family. Wyatt's last wife, Josephine Sarah "Sadie" Earp, described Virginia Ann in her memoirs:

"Wyatt's mother was a Southern woman with a soft Southern voice; hospitality and love radiated from every part of her. What Wyatt loved, she loved, and a whole world besides. Her life was full of kittens, puppies, birds, little wild animals that came to be fed, ragamuffins, the livestock on the place that all came to her like pets, her menfolks and their women and children, plus anyone and anything in need of help or encouragement. If they were hurt or sick, all the more reason to love and tend them."[6]

Family members may have regarded Virginia Ann as sweet, kind and gentle. But, as daughter Adelia Edwards recalled in her memoirs, Mother Earp could be pretty tough too.

Adelia's recollections of her pipe-smoking mom include a rather painful experience in 1877, when the daughter was 16.

"Our parents were very strict with us about certain things. We had to be polite to visitors and I sure did catch a hot one day in Dodge. Mr. Kelly, the mayor, called on us and there was no doubt but that he was drunk. He was red in the face and he swayed just a little and he really could not get his words right. I don't recall exactly but I can just see him talking to mother now.

Warren and Morg were there, sitting down. The mayor said something like ' I was hoping Mr. Earp would be here.' Well, it was quite obvious he was not there, but the mayor sort of said it as if he was there right in front of him. And then it all happened so quick. Warren said, in a whisper 'What's he talking about?' to Morg. Morg said very quickly, from a newspaper, ' A belly full of booze or sunstroke,' and he winked at me. Well, I just laughed and before I knew it I said to Morg, ' He's drunk as a skunk.'

Now the conversation just went on awhile and I breathed a sigh of relief. I thought they had not noticed. After a while, the mayor and Morg and Warren went out and mother sort of casually said to me. 'Young lady, I'm going to have to teach you to act your age.' And she went to the closet where the switch was kept. It was no use arguing with my parent about things like that. I laid foreword over the arm of a chair, mother made the arrangements to me and then a dozen mighty licks of that long old switch had me on fire.

That was not long before we (Adelia and William Edwards) were getting married and it was the last and worse whipping I ever did get. I couldn't sit for a day and I had extra chores to do for a week. But there was no whining about it after [wards]. We just took our medicine in them days."[7]

Virginia Ann Cooksey Earp died on January 14, 1893, at the age of 72 and was laid to rest at Pioneer Cemetery in San Bernardino.

The *San Bernardino Daily Courier* had this to say about the beloved Earp mom the next day:
"Mrs. Earp, the wife of N.P. Earp of Colton,

departed this life on Saturday and will be buried today at 2 P.M. at Colton. Mrs. Earp is one of the pioneer ladies of this county and was a most estimable lady. She leaves a large circle of friends who will deeply mourn her loss. The Courier extends its heartfelt sympathy to the bereaved husband who, in his old age has lost the companion of his life, the one who has always been true and faithful to him. May she rest in peace."[8]

The headstone of Virginia Ann Cooksey Earp in the Pioneer Cemetery in San Bernardino, CA. From the author's collection.

Zach Earp, left, Mayor of Colton Deirdre Bennett, center, Don Earp on right. Dedication of new grave marker for Virginia Earp in 2002. Author's collection.

Virginia Ann's grave marker had been missing for years and, as a result, the exact location of her internment is not certain. Fortunately, the E.A.R.P. Society acquired a headstone and a memorial ceremony was held at Pioneer Cemetery on January 12, 2002.[9]

"DEELIE"
ADELIA (EARP) EDWARDS

Adelia Douglas (Earp) Edwards, the youngest of the Earp children and the only daughter who lived until adulthood, was born in Pella, Iowa on June 16, 1861. "Deelie" as everyone called her, was only three years old when her family arrived in San Bernardino on December 17, 1864. They all went back to the Midwest in 1868—with the exception of Wyatt, Virgil and Jim—returned once more to Southern California in 1877.

The California bound Earps made their first home in Temescal, near the present day city of Corona. The following "homesick" letter written by Morgan's wife, Louisa to her sister, Agnes, gives some insight on the period when the California bound Earps lived there. The original correspondence is in the Glenn G. Boyer collection and a copy was given to the late San Bernardino/Earp historian, Fred Holladay.

> "Temescal, California
> March the 5th, 1880
>
> Dear Sister Agnes,
>
> I again take my pen in hand to let you know where I am. We arrived at San Bernardino on

Adelia Earp Edwards, sister of the Earp boys.
From the Boyer Collection.

Wednesday evening and on Thursday we came by train to the Temescal Mountains warm springs. It is a very pretty place to live and I suppose I will have to live here now for some time for there is no way to make enough to away. I am so far from the states now that I feel as though I shall not get back again. They are all very old fashioned people here and I like it very much. They have a nice bath house where the warm water runs out of the mountain, and a orchard of lemons and oranges. The trees are full of lemons but the oranges are all gathered. The peach trees are all in bloom and everything is green and there is so many wild flowers. I have been out gathering some to press. It is a hotel for the people to come to the springs that are sick. There is fourteen rooms, but there is no sick people here now because they say it is too cold weather. The people in this country don't know what cold weather is. They say it snowed two inches here this winter. The people that have lived here for twenty years never saw any snow here before.

It is thirty miles to San Bernardino. I have got a chance to send my letter to town so I must close. Give my love to all my people and tell Boshford to write. Give this money to mother, so good-bye, from your sister Louisa Houston to Agnes Houston."[10]

During the latter part of 1880, the Earps moved a few miles southwest of San Bernardino and settled in the small town of Colton. From that point on, Adelia lived in the San Bernardino area until shortly before her death in 1941.[11]

The Earp Clan was a close knit family as Adelia attested:

"I guess I had a real happy childhood, in many places, and even when I married young, I was close to my folks for the rest of their lives. I can never tell how I felt when mother died. She died in 1893. I was sick for days and ill for weeks after [wards]. It just seemed like there could not be a world without her and I reckon I'll miss her until I go too. That was forty years gone [ago] and I have thought of her every day since. My father [Nicholas] was a fine man."[12]

Adelia's memoirs have been a valuable source of information regarding her famous family and especially for a personal analysis of her brothers.

She described the Earp boys when they were in their thirties:

> "Wyatt and Virgil were not too much alike in nature. Wyatt and Jim were more alike, and Morg and Warren were too. Virgil was Virgil and there wasn't nobody much like him. He was a fine man. He was the biggest and had a big booming voice and laugh and a real big heart too. You would really have to push him some to make him angry but then he really did explode. I guess Wyatt and Jim were the same that way, like mother too, and me, I reckon. Morg and Warren were like my father more, they were quicker tempered boys. Only Newton and Warren were dark like my father, the other boys favored my mother and were fair."[13]

Adelia married William Thomas Edwards (1856-1919) and had nine children: Mary, Leroy, Nicholas Virgil, Estelle, Helena, George, Myrl, Florence, and Raymond.[14]

Bill appeared to be a hard worker—holding down jobs at various times as a citrus rancher, carpenter and church sexton—but for whatever reasons, the Edwards never seemed to stay put very long. They lived at a number of locations in the San Bernardino Valley—Colton, San Bernardino, Mentone, Highland, East Highlands and Yucaipa. When daughter, Estelle, was born in 1887, they were living in Colton. But two years later, they were residing on Rousseau Alley in San Bernardino.[15]

The *San Bernardino Weekly Times-Index* for October 20, 1898, reported a rather alarming incident involving Bill, while he and Adelia were living in Yucaipa:

> "William T. Edwards had the misfortune last Thursday to let a fire get the best of him while he was engaged in burning some brush on his home farm. The wind came up from the northwest at a lively rate at about 11:30 and carried the fire into some heavy brush and pine timber, and soon the whole side of the mountain was a solid sheet of blaze. It swept the timber from P.E. Covington's ranch clean and burned some on the government park. The damage will foot up to the sum of $1,000. At this writing the fire is still burning."[16]

The following letters written by "Grandpa" Nicholas and "Mother" Adelia to her son Leroy at the time of his 13th birthday in November, 1898 shows the close ties and concerns for their family. The ever so cautious (and somewhat incoherent writer) Nick wrote:

> "My Dear grandson you are young and your feet are in the slippery paths of youth and you are liable to slip stumble and fall never to rais again now take warning by one that wishes you well be on your gard for there is many snare(?) gins and strategins(?) set to ensnare you from the right way Be watchful and shirk(?).... From your old grand Father N.P. Earp 85 years old"

Adelia's letter is a bit more soothing.

"November 6, 1898...Dear Son When this you
See Remember me and ever bear in mind that
I will be your friend to you when others Seem
Unkind....From your Mother A.D. Edwards".

After Leroy married Sue Bessant on October 12,
1907, they settled down in San Bernardino and eventually bought a house on 1275 Belle Street. During his
family visits, Wyatt stopped by Leroy and Sue's home a
number of times. The house is still standing today.[17]

In 1906, the Edwards family was back in San Bernardino and living on the north side of Base Line
Street, east of Waterman Avenue. There apparently
was a big family-owned ranch in that area at the time.
Ninety-year-old Al Bessant recalled that his grandfa-
ther, James Bessant had a 30-40 acre spread on Baseline

*Sue (Bessant) and Leroy Edwards at their home on Belle Street in San
Bernardino. From the Al Bessant Collection.*

in close proximity to the Edwards' home. At least two other Bessant families moved nearby and according to the 1906 San Bernardino City Directory, there were eight "Bessants" listed. But what really turned this into a "family affair" is that Al Bessant is also the nephew of Leroy Edwards, and a direct link with the Earp clan.[18]

After Virgil died in 1905, his wife, Allie, moved in with the Edwards on Base Line in San Bernardino. The two sisters-in-law would become lifelong best friends and live under the same roof until shortly before Adelia's death.

Earp Family gathering at the Bessant Ranch on Baseline east of Waterman Avenue. From the Al Bessant Collection.

In an unpublished manuscript, Earp Historian Glenn Boyer wrote:

"Allie used to ask Adelia, who was closer to her than a sister, to walk with her in the lonesome twilight and help her get over her 'grieven'...She never did."

Mrs. Virgil Earp (Aunt Allie), left with her dear friend, Adelia Earp Edwards (the Earp boys' sister), at the time they saw Randolph Scott playing Wyatt Earp in Frontier Marshall, and agreed that his poker faced rendition of Wyatt was true-to-life. From the Boyer Collection.

A few years later, Adelia and Bill moved several miles further east to East Highlands. In an article for the San Bernardino County Museum Association (Winter, 1973), entitled "My Recollections of East Highlands: 1908-1920", Alice Van Boven wrote:

"The Bill Edwards family lived in one of the little houses Mr. Benson built, about 1909 to 1911. I did not know at the time that Mrs. Edwards was the former Adelia Earp, sister of Virgil and Wyatt. For a while, her brother, James and his wife lived in a tent beside their house. It was then that Father asked if they were related to Wyatt. I never heard them mention Wyatt or Virgil, although 'Aunt Allie', Virgil's wife used to come see them. Their were five Edwards children; the oldest, Mrs. Boren was living elsewhere; she had two children. Myrl was out of school—Raymond and Florence were in school, and George, too young for school. Florence saw from only one eye because as a baby she had stuck Raymond's pocket knife into her eye--she told us her Mother had thrown the knife away. George used to play dolls with Florence and us. Mr. Edwards was a carpenter."[19]

The Edwards were back in San Bernardino and living at 1330 Lugo Street (now Lugo Avenue) when Bill died on May 30, 1919, of a cerebral hemorrhage at the age of 63. It was a tough loss and a hard time for Adelia and the family.

Bill's obituary in the *San Bernardino Sun* the next day paid a glowing tribute to the man:

"William Thomas Edwards died last evening at 8:45 o'clock, at his home 1330 Lugo Street. He had been ill for but a week or so, and his passing came as a shock to the family. He was 63 years old, and a native of Missouri, having come to California 42 years ago from the east. He was well known by the older residents of the city and valley, and will be sorely missed in his circle of friends, as well as in the home, where he was greatly beloved as a man accustomed to doing the little deeds of kindness which count for so much in everyday life. He had been the sexton in Pioneer cemetery for some time.

Beside the widow, Mrs. Adelia Edwards,

Adelia and husband Bill lived in this house on D Street in San Bernardino. From Author's collection.

there remain five daughters and three sons, Mrs. H.L. Boren, Mrs. W.F. Miller, Mrs. Gus Boren, Mrs. L.T. Sullivan, and Miss Florence Edwards, and Virgil Edwards, Leroy Edwards, and George Edwards, all of this city."[20]

Adelia moved again shortly after her husband's death. The 1920 City Directory for San Bernardino lists Addia (Sic) D. Edwards, widow of William T. Edwards, as residing at 1068 "D" Street.[21]

But when her brother, Wyatt died in 1929, his obituary mentioned that the widowed Adelia Edwards was residing in Highland. The *San Bernardino Daily Sun* for January 14, 1929 reported:

"Two Gun Man of West Dies

He had been suffering from kidney trouble for three years. His widow, Mrs. Sadie Earp, and a sister, Mrs. W. Edwards of Highland, California, survive him."[21]

During her last years, Adelia stayed with her daughter, Myrl (Edwards) Sullivan at 1535 East 82nd Street in Los Angeles. She passed away there at 10:15 P.M. on January 16, 1941, at the age of 79 from Hypostatic Pneumonia.

Adelia is buried alongside her husband and brother Jim at Mountain View Cemetery in San Bernardino. When Allie died at the age of 98 in1947, Adelia's daughters had her ashes buried in an urn atop their mother's coffin.[23]

Adelia Edwards' grave in Mountain View Cemetery in San Bernardino. Author's Collection.

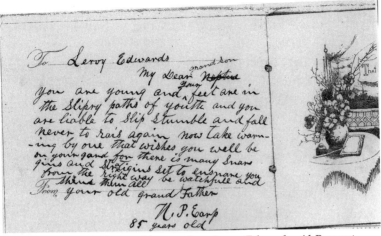

Letter from Nick Earp to his grandson Leroy Edwards. Al Bessant Collection.

Letter from Adelia to her son Leroy Edwards. Al Bessant Collection.

END NOTES

1. Boyer, Glenn G., *I Married Wyatt Earp*, p. 137, 1976.
2. Holladay, Fred, "The Earp Clan in San Bernardino County", *Heritage Tales*, pp. 21- 22, 1978.
3. Rousseau, Sarah Jane, Rousseau Diary, 1864.
4. Boyer, Glenn G., *I Married Wyatt Earp*, p. 37, 1976.
5. "He Died With His Boots On", *San Bernardino Daily Sun*, July 10, 1900.
6. Boyer, Glenn G., *I Married Wyatt Earp*, p. 130, 1976.
7. Edwards, Adelia, Memoirs, p. 7, written in 1932-1934, copyright, David H. Cruickshanks, Colton City Library, 1978.
8. Obituary, *San Bernardino Courier* 1/15/93.
9. Pioneer Cemetery Records, San Bernardino, Ca.
10. Houston, Louisa, letter written to her sister, Agnes. The original correspondence is in the Glenn G. Boyer collection and a copy was given to the late San Bernardino/Earp historian, Fred Holladay in 1984.
11. Record of Funeral for Adelia Douglas Edwards, January 16, 1941.
12. Edwards, Adelia, *Memoirs*, p. 8, written in 1932-1934, copyright David H. Cruickshanks, 1978.
13. Edwards, Adelia, *Memoirs*, p. 11, written in 1932-1934, copyright David H. Cruickshanks, 1978.
14. Genealogy of William Thomas Edwards, Norman Feldheym Central Library's "California Room", San Bernardino, Ca.
15. "Estelle Josephine Miller, Wyatt Earp's Niece, Dies", *San Bernardino Sun*, (newspaper) May 8, 1968.
16. *San Bernardino Weekly Times Index*, (newspaper) October 20, 1898.
17. Bessant, Al, Oral interview, August, 2003 and May, 2006.
18. IBID.

19. Boven, Alice Van, "My Recollections of East Highlands: 1908--1920, *San Bernardino County Museum Association Quarterly, Winter, 1973*. James' wife, Bessie, died in 1887. Alice Boven must have assumed that Jame's wife was with him.

20. Obituary, William Thomas Edwards, *San Bernardino Sun* (newspaper), May 31, 1919.

21. 1920 San Bernardino City Directory.

22. Obituary for Wyatt Earp, *San Bernardino Sun*, (newspaper), January 14, 1929.

23. Record of Funeral for Adelia Douglas Edwards, January 16, 1941.

Chapter Nine

REDISCOVERING WYATT EARP'S DESERT CAMPSITE

So much has been written about Wyatt Earp and the time he spent in Wichita, Dodge City, and Tombstone. On the other hand, hardly anything is ever mentioned about his "Happy Days Mine" desert campsite located out in the remote southeastern corner of the Mojave Desert. This was home to Wyatt and his wife, Sadie, for about twenty years. It is this little publicized episode in Wyatt's life that had intrigued me for a long time.[1]

Fortunately, I met up with Mike Stubbs during the spring of 1995. My new friend and link to Wyatt Earp's past was at the time a business man-

Wyatt Earp, c. 1926, at the time he was working with John H. Flood, Jr. on his life story. Glenn Boyer Collection.

ager at Crest Chevrolet in San Bernardino. He was also someone who shared the same interest and desire that I've had for delving into this little known aspect in the life of one of the most identifiable men in the history of the Old West.

Mike, who has had a good deal of prospecting experience dating back to 1958, and his son Brett, had a general idea where the Earp's campsite was located from maps of that portion of the Mojave Desert showing a small section of land labeled as the "Lucky Day Mine". They decided to not only find the mine, but to devote a day attempting to locate specifically where the campsite was as well.[2]

For reference as they scouted around trying to relocate the old campsite, Mike and Brett used a photograph of Wyatt and Sadie standing in front of their tent cabin taken from Bob Boze Bell's *The Illustrated Life and Times of Wyatt Earp*. They were excited by the fact that somewhere out in that quiet and unmolested desert Wyatt and Sadie slept, ate, and talked with friends for months at a time over a span of 20 years. Yet, with all that has been written and hyped up about Wyatt, and with all the places that Earp enthusiasts have visited, quite possibly nobody in recent times had actually gone to the campsite.

One early Saturday morning Mike and Brett started out in search of the campsite. Using maps and the photograph as guides, they traveled half-way between Vidal Junction and the California/Arizona border, along Highway 62. Then they put Mike's Suburban 4 by 4 to the test by taking off cross-country on some rugged dirt roads in hopes of finding the mine. Finally, after a couple hours in which they scoped out several miles of land, they came upon an abandoned telephone road which led them to one of the mine's entrances. Soon two more entrances were found, one of which still had the remains of rail used for hauling out the ore.

After a couple hours looking inside the mine, Mike and Brett set out to find Wyatt and Sadie's campsite— their primary goal. Now that the father and son team had a reference point, they used their experience in desert traveling and camping in trying to figure out where Wyatt and Sadie would have set up their camp. Mike and Brett drove in a northwest direction. Feeling pretty certain that the campsite wouldn't be more than 1,000 feet or so from the mine, they stopped and turned to the northeast. Then they headed south and

Wyatt Earp's Camp, the site near present day Vidal Junction, CA, where his Happy Day Mine group was located, showing the tent/cabin where Wyatt and Sadie stayed. The Boyer Collection.

finally north toward the aqueduct around 4:30 P.M.

Eventually Mike and Brett got out of their vehicle and took off on foot. Splitting up, they looked around arroyos and washes. While Brett was walking, he continued looking at the campsite picture in *Life and Times of Wyatt Earp*, trying to visualize where that picture was taken. While Mike was digging out of the ground what appeared to be an old rusted oil drum, Brett stood about seventy yards away standing on top of a bluff, gazing with exuberance at the photograph once again.

Suddenly he yelled out, "Dad, get here quick. I found it!"

Looking toward another bluff across from where they were standing, Mike and Brett were able to see the same volcanic rock outcropping exactly as shown in the photograph! Peering down, they saw the campsite. The trees in the photograph were still standing. Oddly enough, the Earps' tent that was shown in the picture appeared to be located in what now is a wash, although it may have been on higher ground at the time the Earps lived there.

Later that day as the sun was setting, Mike and Brett thought about the many sunsets Wyatt and Sadie probably enjoyed at that camp. Now, many years later, they were alone at the very spot enhancing the same experience.[3]

A short time after this exploration I was introduced to Mike Stubbs through my good friend, Russ Mc Donald. After hearing about their find, Mike and I immediately made plans to go out to the site again. In April, the two of us along with another friend, Wayne Heaton, set out for Wyatt and Sadie's desert home.

Upon arrival at the old campsite I noticed an old trash dump that appeared to have not been disturbed for quite some time. Included in the dump were some old rusted cans, a flour sifter, tobacco cans, an old oil drum, broken bottles and plates.

Wyatt Earp's Camp, tent and ramada with Sadie at left, Wyatt at right, and the ever present dog. Discovered in Sadie Earp's private papers. The Boyer Collection.

I was excited to think that we were holding things that Wyatt and Sadie may have actually used at their campsite.

Soon Mike, Wayne and I found more important evidence that this was the right location. We spotted a rock ledge built partially around a tree and the remains of an old tree house. Although she didn't specify this location in her memoirs which were collected and edited by Glenn Boyer in his book, *I Married Wyatt Earp*, Sadie spoke of a tree house that Wyatt and Jim built for

Wyatt's desert campsite in 1995. Author's collection.

her. We wondered if this was the site that she was talking about. We enjoyed our thoughts of Sadie and Wyatt playing here like kids, not a thought most people put with Wyatt.[4]

L. to R. Bob Boze Bell, Mike Stubbs, Jay Cataldo (5-years-old) and author, Nick Cataldo, at Wyatt's camp site in 1995. Bob Boze Bell is the Editor of True West Magazine and a commentator on Encore Westerns cable channel. Author's collection.

One of mine entrances to Happy Day mines, 1995. Author, left, with Mike Stubbs. Author's Collection.

While many might question the importance of this "rediscovery" of the Happy Days Gold Mine campsite, the real significance in exploring this site is that virtually nothing has been written about Wyatt's stay here despite the fact that the man spent more of his life here than the more publicized settings such as Dodge City and Tombstone. In addition, much information regarding those more well-known locations and events in Wyatt's life was very likely discussed at this site. Thousands of people visit these well known "Earp towns" each year and absorb the multitude of available rehashed information about Wyatt at various museums, and tourist sites. Yet, here in the remote southeastern corner of the Mojave Desert is about as close as anyone can be to a place where Wyatt Earp spent so much of his time—a place virtually untouched since the day he left about 70 years earlier. We felt like this "rediscovery" could be compared to someone finding Kit Carson's knapsack inside a cave while innocently sitting nearby under a tree having lunch.

As we headed back home, I thought about how so few people knew that the legendary Wyatt Earp spent many years working as a miner in this remote corner of San Bernardino County and how the vast amount of time he spent here far out balanced the few years he spent as a lawman. Then I asked myself two questions regarding Wyatt Earp... the desert miner.

(1) Would thousands of people flock annually to the hot, desolate Mojave Desert in order to visit the former home of a miner grub staking in the dry mountains of the Mojave Desert? and (2), would Hugh O'Brian or Henry Fonda have been willing to play the lead as they did in television and movie roles?

It didn't take long for me to come up with the answers... probably not!

As with most of our heroes, we are drawn to romance and excitement of their lives, not the day to day existence of just plain living. However, with these discoveries, Wyatt has begun to emerge as a real live three dimensional person, not just a larger than life character in a dime novel or a celluloid image on the silver screen.

END NOTES

1. Boyer, Glenn G., *I Married Wyatt Earp*, 1976.
2. Stubbs, Michael, Oral Interview, 1995.
3. Bell, Bob Boze, *The Illustrated Life and Times of Wyatt Earp*, 3rd edition, 1995.
4. Boyer, Glenn G., *I Married Wyatt Earp*, 1976.

Chapter Ten

EARPS AND CLANTONS
IN SAN BERNARDINO

ॐ

Old West enthusiasts living in Southern California's San Bernardino County might be surprised to find out that the legendary silver mining town of Tombstone, Arizona and Southern California's San Bernardino County have a rather unique bond.

Richard Gird teamed up with the Schieffellin brothers in 1878 to lay the foundation of Tombstone. Several years later, he moved to Southern California's San Bernardino County and helped put the city of Chino on the map.[1]

Indian agent, John P. Clum, who became mayor of the famed "Town Too Tough to Die" as well as the first editor of the *Tombstone Epitaph*, eventually moved on to San Bernardino in 1886, where he busily engaged in the real estate and insurance business.[2]

The Frink family were prominent early San Bernardino Valley residents. George Frink later became a stage coach driver in and around Tombstone.[3]

There was even a San Bernardino Ranch in southeastern Arizona.

The most ironic twist of all is that the Earps and the Clantons may have known each other long before the two names would become immortalized in history together at the so-called "Gunfight at the O.K. Corral."

Upon arriving in San Bernardino after a seven month long wagon trek from the Midwest in December of 1864, Nick Earp and his family (including 16-year-old Wyatt) rented a farm from a rancher named Carpenter a short distance from the Santa Ana River in what is now part of Redlands. They were to roost there for the next three years.[4]

Newman Haynes (Old Man) Clanton was co-leader of the Cowboy gang (his sons and the McLaury boys) that clashed with the Earps and Doc Holladay in Tombstone. He and his family lived in San Timoteo Canyon for a while during the 1860s and may have been acquainted with the Earps at that time. The Boyer Collection.

Meanwhile, Newman "Old Man" Clanton and his crew moved around Southern California. According to the memoirs of San Bernardino Valley pioneer William Frink, the Clantons settled in for a spell as tenant farmers in nearby San Timoteo Canyon sometime between 1865 and 1867.[5]

Frink recalled that brother George attended San Timoteo School with Ike Clanton and coincidentally ended up driving stages between Tombstone and Benson. Therefore, if the information is accurate, he knew the Clantons from both San Bernardino and Tombstone.[6]

In Billy Breakenridge's autobiography Helldorado, a "Mr. Frink" helped a posse which included Wyatt and Virgil Earp, chase Apaches in 1881 just before the celebrated shootout. It can be assumed here that George Frink was the "Mr. Frink", then he knew the Earps well too.[7]

Ike Clanton, major player in the "Cowboy Gang". He may have known the Earps while living in Southern California. The Boyer Collection.

To my knowledge, there is still no proof that any of the Earps and Clantons ever actually met during their San Bernardino days. However, since there weren't a whole lot of people living in that part of the valley and both clans were farming in close proximity to each other, it is quite possible that some of the families' members crossed paths at one time or another.

Who knows? They all may have been friends at one time. Or perhaps a long time family feud reached the boiling point early in the afternoon of October 26, 1881, when gunshots rang out in the vicinity of Third and Fremont Streets in Tombstone.

END NOTES

1. Brown, John Jr., and Boyd, James, *History of San Bernardino and Riverside Counties*, p.238, 1922.

2. Assessors book for San Bernardino County, 1886.

3. Frink, William H., *Old Martinez Ranch* (unpublished), 1937.

4. Flood, John Henry Jr., *Biography of Wyatt Earp* (unpublished and edited by Earl Chafin Press), 1926.

5. Written Correspondences between Sue C. Van Slyke and Arda M. Haenszel, 1991. Mrs. Van Slyke did extensive research on the Clanton family which resulted in articles written for Quarterly of the *National Association and Center for Outlaw and Lawman History* entitled "Kin to the Clantons" and "The Truth about the Clantons of Tombstone."

6. Frink, William H., *Old Martinez Ranch* (unpublished), 1937.

7. Breakenridge, William M., Helldorado, pp. 274-276, 1928.

BIBLIOGRAPHY

Newspapers

Arizona Prospector, (newspaper), November 11, 1893.

Belden, L. Burr, "History In the Making", San Bernardino Sun-Telegram, April 23, 1956.

Belden, L. Burr, "Wyatt Earp's Desert Home Saved For Public", San Bernardino Sun - Telegram (newspaper), June 25, 1961.

Calico Print, (newspaper) May 3, 1885.

Hartley, Seth, "War Between Colton and San Bernardino..." Colton Courier, June 1, 1939.

Holladay, Fred, quotes from the San Bernardino Daily Times for January 1, 1878.)

Holladay, Fred, quotes from the San Bernardino Daily Times, newspaper, April 29, 1878)

Mauel, Ed., "Orange Show Blossoms in Book", San Bernardino Sun, July 31, 1994.

Needles Nugget (newspaper), "Earp of Old Frontier Dies" January 18, 1929.

Obituary, San Bernardino Courier 1/15/93.

October 14 issue of the Daily Times.

Riverside Press and Horticulturist (newspaper), August 11, 1883.

San Bernardino Daily Courier, newspaper, January 15, 1893.

San Bernardino Daily Sun,"He Died With His Boots On", July 10, 1900.

San Bernardino Sun, (newspaper)"Estelle Josephine Miller, Wyatt Earp's Niece, Dies", May 8, 1968.

San Bernardino Times - Index, (newspaper), August 18, 1893.

San Bernardino Times-Index, April 28, 1893.

San Bernardino Weekly Courier, December 3, 1892.

San Bernardino Weekly Times (newspaper), October 16, 1880, reprinted from

San Bernardino Weekly Times Index, (newspaper) October 20, 1898.

San Bernardino Weekly Times, newspaper, July 27, 1878.

San Bernardino Weekly Times, p.7, September 30, 1892.

San Francisco News letter and California Advertiser (newspaper), April 2, 1892.

San Jacinto Valley Register, (newspaper), May 1, 1953.

Saulsbury, James M., "Famed Earp Family Well-Known in San Bernardino Area", San Bernardino Sun, April 17, 1957.

Sheffield, Larry, "Why Did Virgil Earp Resign?" San Bernardino Sun, p. B7, August 7, 2005.

The Oregonian (newspaper) for April 22, 1899, mentions about Virgil's reunion with his daughter. Obituary from the Oregonian (newspaper), October 24, 1905.

The San Bernardino Daily Index, newspaper, November 27, 1881.

The San Bernardino Guardian, newspaper, November 9, 1867.

The San Bernardino Sun, newspaper, February 2, 1907, p.6.

The San Bernardino Weekly Times, newspaper, October 16, 1886.

San Bernardino Guardian (newspaper), May 23, 1868, p. 2, col. 1.

San Bernardino Guardian, (newspaper), February 24, 1872.

Government Documents

15-132, Examining physician's report dated January 2, 1884.

Assessors book for San Bernardino County, 1886.

Census for San Bernardino County, July 23, 1880.

Colton Board of Trustees, Proceedings, pp. 1-2, July 25, 1887.

Death certificate and Pension records (1912) for Newton J. Earp.

Department of Health, Certificate Copy of Local Record of Death of James Cooksey Earp. April 6,1926.

Edited by Stanley W. Paher, Las Vegas: Nevada Publications, 1976, pp. 319--320.

Examining Surgeon's Certificate, October 21, 1874.

Great Register for San Bernardino County, May 5, 1879.

Great Register of Voters for May 12, 1880 and the Temescal census for June 29, 1880.

Great Voter Registration, 1908.

Land Deed (copy) for Virgil Earp, San Bernardino's Norman Feldheym Central Library, July 7, 1888.

National Archives, Washington D.C., File WC

Official death records, Riverview Cemetery Association, Portland, Oregon, October 25, 1905.

San Bernardino City Directory, 1987.

San Bernardino County Archives, Index to mines and Deeds for Wyatt and Josephine Earp.

San Bernardino County Courts, Waymire and Trona trial manuscripts.

San Bernardino County Directories, 1914, 1920, and 1924.

San Bernardino County Directory, 1887.

San Bernardino County Supervisor Minutes, Book D, p. 432.

State of Nevada, County of Esmeralda, Oath of Office, signed

June 26, San Bernardino's Norman Feldheym Central Library 1905.

The San Bernardino County Supervisor Minutes, Book D, p. 432.

U.S. Pension records, Declaration for Pension of James C. Earp, May 1, 1920.

Periodicals

Atwood, G.A., San Bernardino in the 1860's, reminiscing speech given to San Bernardino Lions Club in 1935, reprinted in *Odyssey*, 1979.

Boyer, Glenn G., Wyatt Earp: Legendary American, (series) True West Magazine, 1993.

Fisk, O.J., as told to Philip Johnston, "Treasures from Vanderbilt," Westways, June, 1952.

King, A.M. as told to Lea F. McCarty, "Wyatt Earp's Million Dollar Shotgun Ride," True West, August 1958, p.p16-17.

Stephenson, Ed, "The Horton Grand; Time Warp in the Gas Lamp", San Diego Magazine, October, 1986. pp. 114-116.

Smith, Dr. Gerald A., San Bernardino County Museum Association Quarterly, Vol. VI, winter, 1958.

Books

Bell, Bob Boze, The Illustrated Life and Times of Wyatt Earp, 3rd edition, Tri Star-Boze Publications, Inc., 1995.

Boyer, Glenn G., I Married Wyatt Earp, University of Arizona Press, 1976.

Boyer, Glenn G., Wyatt Earp's Tombstone Vendetta, Talei Publishers, Inc., 1993.

Chafin, Earl, "Wyatt's Woman (She Married Wyatt Earp), The Earl Chafin Press, edited 1998.

Breakenridge, William M., *Helldorado*, Houghton-Mifflin Co., 1928.

Brown, John Jr., and Boyd, James, History of San Bernardino and Riverside Counties, The Lewis Publishing Company, 1922.

Casebier, Dennis G., The Battle of Camp Cady, Dennis G. Casebier, 1972.

Chaput, Don, Earp Papers, Affiliated Writers of America Inc., 1994.

Chaput, Don, Virgil Earp: Western Peace Officer, Affiliated Writers of America, Inc., 1994.

Cilch, Kenneth R., Sr., Wyatt Earp; The Missing Years, Gaslamp

Books/Museum, 1998.

Edwards, Jean Whitten, Earp Family Genealogy, Breckenridge, Texas: Beck Printing, 1991.

Holladay, Fred, "As Rich as Vanderbilt", Heritage Tales, City of San Bernardino Historical and Pioneer Society, 1979.

Holladay, Fred, "The Earp Clan in San Bernardino County", Heritage Tales, City of San Bernardino Historical and Pioneer Society, 1978.

Holladay, Fred, "Warren Earp: The Tragic One", Heritage Tales, City of San Bernardino Historical and Pioneer Society, 1979.

Holladay, Fred, The Earp Brothers in Goldfield, in Nevada Official Bicentennial Book, 1904.

Ingersoll, L.A., Century Annals of San Bernardino County 1769 to 1904, L. A. Ingersoll, 1904.

Hickey, Michael M., The Death of Warren Baxter Earp: A Closer Look, Talei Publishers, Inc., 2000.

Lake, Stuart N., Wyatt Earp: Frontier Marshal, Houghton Mifflin Co., 1931.

Maltsberger, Elma, The Story of Colton (Letter from Nick Earp to James Copla), Elma Maltsberger, 1974.

Miller, Nyle H. and Snell, Joseph W., Great Gunfighters of The Kansas Cowtowns: 1867-1886, University of Nebraska Press, 1963.

Silva, Lee A., Wyatt Earp-A biography of the Legend: Vol. 1, The Cowtown Years, Graphic Publishers, 2002.

Tefertiller, Casey, Wyatt Earp: The Life Behind the Legend, John Wiley and Sons, Inc., 1997.

Traywick, Ben T., The Chronicles of Tombstone, Red Marie's Bookstore, 1986.

Turner, Alford E., The O.K. Corral Inquest, Creative Publishing Co., 1981.

Unpublished Manuscripts

Boyer, Glenn G., unpublished manuscript, Colton Public Library, pp. 12-13.

Edwards, Adelia, Memoirs, copyright, David H. Cruickshanks, Colton City Library, 1978.

Flood, John Henry Jr., Biography of Wyatt Earp (unpublished and edited by Earl Chafin Press), 1926.

Frink, William H., Old Martinez Ranch (unpublished), 1937.

Genealogy of William Thomas Edwards, Norman Feldheym

Central Library's "California Room", San Bernardino, Ca.
Hanna, Wilson, written statement (undated), Colton City Library.
Houston, Louisa, letter written to her sister, Agnes. The original correspondence is in the Glenn G. Boyer collection and a copy was given to the late San Bernardino/Earp historian, Fred Holladay in 1984.
Rousseau, Sarah Jane, Rousseau Diary, 1864.
San Bernardino Public Library, Holman Curtis recollections, undated.
Turner, Alford E. and Oster, William W., Colton's Marshal Earp, Colton Public Library.

Interviews
Bessant, Al, Oral interview, August, 2003 and May, 2006.
Clyde, Robert, Oral interview with author, 1990.
Daggett, Nathalie, Oral Interview with Marsha Patrick, 1993.
Molony, Richard, Oral Interview, 1998.
Petersen, Jim, Oral interview, June 11, 2006.
Sheffield, Larry, Oral interview with author, June, 2004.
Spolidoro, Grace, Oral Interview with author, 1989.
Stubbs, Michael, Oral Interview, 1995.
Traywick, Ben T., Oral interview, May 25, 2006.

Written Correspondence
Van Slyke, Sue C. and Haenszel, Arda M., Written Correspondences, 1991. Mrs. Van Slyke did extensive research on the Clanton family which resulted in articles written for Quarterly of the National Association and Center for Outlaw and Lawman History entitled "Kin to the Clantons" and "The Truth about the Clantons of Tombstone."
Houston,Louisa, letter written to her sister Kate. The original correspondence is in the Glenn G. Boyer collection and a copy was given to the late San Bernardino/Earp historian, Fred Holiday in 1984.

Others
Pioneer Cemetery Records, San Bernardino, Ca.
Record of Funeral for Adelia Douglas Edwards, January 16, 1941.
San Bernardino Society of California Pioneers, Minute Book A, April 28, 1888, p. 45.
San Bernardino Society of California Pioneers, Minute Book B, August 2, 1890, pp. 170,172.

Index